Taking Ideas to Market

Tim Jones and Simon Kirby

T0341953

- Fast track route to successfully taking new ideas to market

- Covers the key areas of innovation, from generating new concepts and selecting the best opportunities to managing a new product launch and ensuring effective delivery

- Examples and lessons from some of the world's most successful businesses, including ABB, eBay, 3M and Zara, and ideas from the smartest thinkers, including Edward de Bono, John Kao, Robert Cooper, Gary Hamel and Clayton Christiansen

- Includes a glossary of key concepts and a comprehensive resources guide

>>EXPRESS EXEC.COM<<
essential management thinking at your fingertips

Taking Ideas to Market

TIM JONES AND SIMON KIRBY

Copyright © Capstone Publishing 2002

The right of Tim Jones and Simon Kirby to be identified as the authors of this work has been asserted in accordance with the Copyright, Designs and Patents Act 1988

First published 2002 by
Capstone Publishing (a Wiley company)
8 Newtec Place
Magdalen Road
Oxford OX4 1RE
United Kingdom
http://www.capstoneideas.com

CIP catalogue records for this book are available from the British Library and the US Library of Congress

ISBN 1-84112-314-5

Contents

Introduction to ExpressExec

ExpressExec is 3 million words of the latest management thinking compiled into 10 modules. Each module contains 10 individual titles forming a comprehensive resource of current business practice written by leading practitioners in their field. From brand management to balanced scorecard, ExpressExec enables you to grasp the key concepts behind each subject and implement the theory immediately. Each of the 100 titles is available in print and electronic formats.

Through the ExpressExec.com Website you will discover that you can access the complete resource in a number of ways:

» printed books or e-books;
» e-content – PDF or XML (for licensed syndication) adding value to an intranet or Internet site;
» a corporate e-learning/knowledge management solution providing a cost-effective platform for developing skills and sharing knowledge within an organization;
» bespoke delivery – tailored solutions to solve your need.

Why not visit www.expressexec.com and register for free key management briefings, a monthly newsletter and interactive skills checklists. Share your ideas about ExpressExec and your thoughts about business today.

Please contact elound@wiley-capstone.co.uk for more information.

Introduction

Why is innovation important? Does it help deliver results? This chapter identifies the benefits from taking more and better ideas to market and provides:

» the context for taking ideas to market; and
» an insight into the changing innovation landscape across industry.

Innovate or die – so has been the mantra for many companies over the past 20 years as they have sought to drive the whole ethos of innovation and continuous improvement throughout their organizations. Especially since the early 80s, firms worldwide have adopted an increasing variety of techniques and approaches to improve their innovation performance and to benefit more from new ideas. Some of these have addressed strategic issues; some the varied processes in use across the company and its network of suppliers and customers; whilst others have focused on core organizational issues such as motivation, reward and structure.

Financial markets reward innovation. A study by Arthur D. Little (a consultancy) found that the top 20% of most innovative firms delivered almost four times the total shareholder returns of the bottom 20% of innovators. Share price includes an element of implied growth, be it organic or by merger and acquisition. The M&A route is perilous – most studies over the last 20 years have found that around 75% of M&A activity fails to create value for shareholders. Organic growth is the alternative to M&A and for this, innovative capability is almost always necessary.

As firms have developed, so the portfolio of approaches to taking ideas to market has itself evolved. As the new economy is brought into line with the old, and the increasing fragmentation of a global economy drives change across multiple sectors, firms operating at the leading edge of the innovation paradigm are adopting a whole new set of approaches to help them redefine the present and build the future. No longer shackled with traditional asset-based economics, companies are increasingly seeing the value of exploiting their intellectual property across multiple sectors, of working with temporary expert networks, of matching equity to brand value, and of introducing a continuous stream of ever-evolving new products and services.

The most significant issue today is the recognition that successfully taking ideas to market is not just invention. Generating ideas is actually the easy bit, efficiently deciding which ones are the best and effectively developing them into competitive products and services is the hard bit. Too many have for too long focused on idea creation and ignored idea selection and idea delivery. Today, in this ever more competitive global environment, succeeding in taking ideas to market has become a capability essential to the future growth of most organizations.

New product development is now a major issue for every developed economy; it is vital to business and wider economic growth. Firms that are successful in innovation secure competitive advantage in rapidly changing world markets, and the economies that generate and support such firms prosper. Innovation is therefore fundamental to stimulating and supporting economic growth and in enabling wealth generation in many industrialized nations. The development of new products and services that can successfully compete in local, national, and global markets has thereby become a key concern for organizations regardless of the sector in which they operate.

Across industries, effective delivery of exciting new ideas has overtaken production efficiency as the key industrial battleground as companies all seek to reduce time to market and to access new technologies in their bid to develop more and better products and services. This is occurring not just in the core manufacturing sectors, but also in service sectors as varied as insurance, waste management, and education. In all fields, the benefits to be attained range from better resource utilization, enhanced productivity, and sustained competitiveness to increased revenue generation and improved shareholder value. Whether involved in the manufacture of discrete products such as consumer goods, medical devices, and industrial machinery, in the production of consumables such as chemicals, paper, and cereals, or in the provision of services such as banking, IT support, and tourism, most organizations are today continuously looking for new opportunities to develop and exploit new or improved products and services.

What is Ideas to Market?

Is invention all that you need, or is there something else as well? This chapter discusses success and failure and highlights aspects of the three key capabilities for taking ideas to market:

» idea creation;
» idea selection; and
» idea delivery.

One brilliant idea is not, by itself, sufficient to bring success to a company. Nor does the adoption of an experimental creative environment ensure any lasting value. An organization focused on innovation and on efficiently developing ideas and launching them into the marketplace does not guarantee profitable revenue streams either. In fact, the successful exploitation of new ideas is not solely concerned with any of:

» being creative and having a good idea;
» seeing a promising opportunity;
» having the resources available to develop an idea;
» efficiently launching a new product into a market; or
» copying what others have done before.

It is all of these. These are some of the essential components of the ability that many organizations aspire to, but which only a select few truly possess. Each of these forms only part of the means by which leading companies deliver exciting new products and services to their customers.

Successfully taking ideas to market is all about having three core capabilities in place and using them together in the most effective and efficient manner. These capabilities are:

» idea creation;
» idea selection; and
» idea delivery.

It is the orchestrated interplay between these three that allows companies like Sony, GE, and Nokia, to consistently out-perform their competitors by being the quickest and the smartest as they grasp new technological opportunities, create new and unique propositions, and continually deliver compelling and competitive new products and services. Companies that do not access all three of these core capabilities are increasingly unlikely to be able to enjoy any significant level of sustained performance in this area. Taking ideas to market is always dependent on all three, and prowess in one or even two of these areas alone is insufficient. While these three core capabilities may not necessarily reside in any one group or even one company, it is the bringing together of these in a synergistic manner that allows leading organizations to successfully deliver new ideas into their chosen markets time after time after time. To create any value from the exploitation of new ideas, organizations have to ensure that these are not only present and in place, but that they are also each given equal significance and are fully aligned.

IDEA CREATION

The first idea is rarely the one that makes it to the final stages of launching a new product or service. It is actually usually pretty unsophisticated. Especially in a world where innovation is becoming the norm, coming up with the incremental next step advance is something that is all too easy and, in turn, is rarely enough to guarantee success. Even if the first thought contains the essence of the final product or service, extensive iteration and continuous modification is frequently required as it gradually evolves into something concrete. More often, however, it is not the first idea that makes it, nor is it the second or the third. These are usually the obvious solutions that many may come up with to a given problem. It is the "non-obvious," the "left-field" concept that is "out of the box" that is needed. Whatever the expression you choose to describe this, you are not after small step, incremental improvement but the big leap forwards. You are after your equivalent of the Walkman, the Post-It, or Viagra, and getting this is certainly not easy.

As the first of the three critical capabilities, idea creation is focused on generating, modifying, building, developing, combining, and refining a wide range of potential ideas, all of which have the potential to solve a problem or provide the world with something new. What is important is generating and developing 100 or even 1000 candidate ideas, and understanding that only one of these will make it. In addition, it is vital to recognize that the first idea will always need development. Whether as an iterative process within one group, or through combining with aspects of existing or other new ideas, building and modifying an idea is essential and therefore has to be accommodated and supported. These are capabilities that cannot be acquired overnight but are, rather, something that individuals, teams, and even organizations can learn and evolve with practice.

There are many issues that are relevant in enabling idea creation to occur successfully, none more so than the underpinning stimulus-motivation-reward environment – within which creativity, innovation, and new thinking can occur. This is not comfy sofas, Coke machines, and big bonuses, but rather the establishment of a culture where risk-taking is encouraged, failure is tolerated, learning is implicit, and recognition and desire for collective team success is paramount. Additionally, team members need to know how to function creatively. Teams full of intelligent, experienced people tend to have highly developed critical faculties. The surest way to kill good ideas is to analyze too robustly, too quickly. Phrases like: "it'll never work because …"; "that's not our core business …"; and "it's been done before by XYZ company and it didn't work" are sure signs of creative failure. Instead, teams need to learn to switch into developmental behaviors at the early stages of idea creation. With such an environment in place, the right people are more easily attracted, a wide range of idea-enabling practices from tools through to attitudes can be introduced, and the beginnings of an idea factory for an organization can be firmly established.

Utilizing whichever techniques are most appropriate, the focus is on generating as many concept solutions as possible and building on them to define multiple combinations of the best elements. The challenge is to not stop at the first apparently good idea, but to continue going forward into a second stage of creativity, questioning but not criticizing so that the candidate list of ideas multiplies in advance of any detailed assessment or evaluation.

IDEA SELECTION

The Ford Edsel, Sinclair C5, Betamax, Persil Color, and Boo.com were all, in principle, good ideas at the time but none ever actually made it in the end. Even though millions of dollars were poured into the development and launch of each of these, they all failed, and failed significantly for a number of arguably pretty basic reasons:

» Ford Edsel – inappropriate visual styling;
» Sinclair C5 – poor configuration and performance;
» Betamax – lack of software availability;

» Persil Color – major side effects; and
» Boo.com – too high level of technology integration.

Idea assessment and selection is concentrated on asking the hard questions up front before significant time and resources are invested, and only then choosing the ones that fully meet the set criteria. Although this sounds simple in theory, in practice what should be a short sharp rational exercise can become very difficult to actually perform. For a start, once any individual or organization has conceived, discussed, and developed what is inevitably considered by its creators to be a good idea, the political and emotional investment is there. Once the train has left the station, there is often no way of even slowing it down, never mind stopping it, until it is far too late. Killing 'babies' is never easy but stopping projects early when they are only ideas is far easier than trying to terminate them later when resources have been invested. This is especially so in companies where poor decision-making and lack of accountability are all too frequent. After they have built up a wealth of candidate opportunities, effective innovators pause for a while and take a hard look at what they have actually got and what they need. Two weeks spent evaluating an idea to make sure it is the right one can easily be made up later, but two weeks not spent ensuring that all the required pieces are in place can easily require six months of rework to fix it later on.

In leading organizations today, effective idea selection involves a series of discrete but interdependent activities, all focused on providing the organization with an objective, unbiased appraisal of the opportunity available, a realistic understanding of whether or not the idea fits with the organization and its ability to deliver and support the associated products and services, and a clear prioritization relative to the alternative propositions available. Such activities commonly include risk analysis, synergy assessment, business case evaluation, market attractiveness and technology availability insights, resource impact analyses, weighted scoring, ranking against value, and cross-portfolio strategy mapping. No matter which of these, or other techniques, are adopted, the fundamental purpose remains to undertake as thorough an assessment as possible up front and thus ensure that subsequent progression into delivery and launch is only enabled for the best, and more significantly, most appropriate ideas.

IDEA DELIVERY

It is all too easy to believe that once an idea has been generated, developed, and chosen as preferential to a host of others, the hard work is over and from here on in it is plain sailing. This common mistake has been the downfall of many individuals, organizations and even national economies as they have failed to recognize the importance of the execution of idea delivery. All too often, good ideas – the microwave oven, MRI, video – have been invented in one country only for another, in these cases Japan, to take up the task of turning these emergent technologies into successful products and thus gaining most from their exploitation. Aware of these and other similar failures to effectively follow through the first steps, more organizations are now also focusing on improving how they actually develop, pilot, test, refine, launch and support new products and services, and thus complete the idea to market journey.

There are three discrete elements involved here which are implicitly interdependent. You can think of them as the three legs of a barstool, where the absence of one renders the whole defunct. Forming the basis of every successful idea delivery capability, these three fundamental elements comprise:

» strategy – the what, the why, and the where;
» process – the how; and
» organization – the who.

Without a clear strategy determining focus and scope, a smooth yet disciplined process ensuring progression, and a motivated and capable team providing the resource, no idea, no matter how exciting, novel, and full of promise, ever fully exploits its true potential, and often never makes it to launch. Time and time again, successful idea delivery has been shown to be influenced by a number of key factors, all of which relate to these three fundamental elements:

» superior, differentiated idea with unique benefits (strategy);
» strong market orientation throughout (strategy);
» sharp, early product definition (strategy);
» quality execution (process);
» multi-functional empowered teams (organization);

» clear decision-making (process);
» well-planned and resourced launch (process);
» correct role for senior management (organization);
» multi-stage and disciplined game plan (process); and
» appropriate structure and governance (organization).

KEY LEARNING POINTS

» Successfully taking ideas to market is about more than creativity. It is about developing the capability to effectively and efficiently create, select, and deliver ideas.
» The idea creation process is about generating, modifying, developing, and refining a wide range of ideas; it make take 100 or even 1000 candidate ideas before recognizing which one will make it.
» A blame-free culture where risk-taking is encouraged, learning is implicit, and collective, team success is paramount. Creative teams also need to be able to temporarily suspend critical judgment and to switch into developmental behaviors.
» Idea selection is best done relatively early before substantial financial and emotional commitments have been made.
» Idea selection generally includes an interlinked assessment of factors such as: risk, synergy and fit, business case evaluation, market attractiveness, technology availability, resource impact, and value and portfolio analysis.
» Idea delivery requires a clear strategy to determine focus and scope, smooth disciplined processes to ensure progression, and a motivated, capable and empowered team.

Evolution of Ideas to Market

Where did this all start and how has that ability of taking ideas to market developed? This chapter explores the origins of the topic, the initial impetus, and recent developments covering:

» the Industrial Revolution;
» early twentieth century issues;
» putting the basics in place;
» globalization and acceleration;
» focus and integration; and
» emerging issues.

At one level, the basic steps in the evolution of humankind, such as the invention of the wheel, could be considered as the first instances of taking ideas to market. For plaudits of the Roman Empire, chariots, pavements, hyper-course systems, galleys, and spas could all justify the claim for this to be the first great period of innovation. Whilst for others, the Ming dynasty in China and the invention of gunpowder and porcelain could be examples of the real emergence of an innovative environment where ideas were first developed and introduced to mass markets. However, for many commentators, the period most associated with the explosion of innovation was the Industrial Revolution that started in the UK in the early eighteenth century.

Why it was in Britain and not France, Italy, or Germany that the Industrial Revolution began has been a source of debate for years, and in his recent book, *The Enlightenment – Britain and the Creation of the Modern World*, Roy Porter identifies a possible explanation: unlike the Catholic cultures of southern Europe or the Calvinistic Dutch, seventeenth century Britain was a place where ideas could be debated in many a different environment. Although fifteenth century Italy had sparked the Renaissance, it was in Britain that the makings of the modern world started. From the London coffee houses, which gave birth to the insurance industry, and where sailors, politicians, playwrights, and merchants would regularly meet and discuss their latest experiences, to establishments like the Royal Society and the Royal Institution, where the great and the good such as Isaac Newton, Michael Faraday and, later, Charles Babbage and friends could regularly debate their most recent theories and discoveries, Britain in the seventeenth century provided the first true cross-functional, multi-disciplinary environment where new ideas could be generated, discussed, debated, enriched, and ultimately exploited. As profession and class have since segregated society, nowhere has the same level of interaction between all walks of life been achieved either by intent or by accident. Even today, in the connected global village of the Internet and the multiproduct multinationals, due to the inherent selection and segregation of skills, interests, and experiences that these artificial forms of social grouping foster, cross-fertilization of ideas between individuals of such varied backgrounds cannot yet be achieved to the same extent as occurred back then.

Supported by such an interactive environment, allowing exchange and development of new ideas, it is not surprising that the invention of iron, steel, steam engines, the railways, the spinning-jenny, cotton mills and paddle-steamers would all follow within a few years. Fuelled by an entrepreneurial spirit and personalities such as James Watt and Richard Arkwright, Britain became the hotbed of innovation, stimulating the rest of the world to follow. However, perhaps more than any other event, the one occasion where ideas from across the world were first truly brought together in one place was the Great Exhibition of 1851 in London. What is now Kensington Gardens and the site of the South Kensington campus of Imperial College, the Royal College of Art, and the Natural History, Science, and Victoria & Albert Museums, was where, for a six-month period, the latest inventions from the US, Europe, and beyond were all brought together for public show. Effectively kick-starting a renewed spurt of innovation, the Great Exhibition can be seen as the point where a major commercial element in taking ideas to market first came into being. Over the next 50 years, as leaders such as Isambard Kingdom Brunel continued to provide inspiration, the creation and delivery of new products and services began to gain a foothold.

However, it was in the twentieth century, with an increasingly lead role from the US, that the manufacture and provision of new products and services really took off. With the advent of Henry Ford's production line for the Model T, the world recognized the real opportunities that were available from having a good idea and exploiting it through introduction into the mass market. Thomas Edison's telephone, George Westinghouse's refrigerators, and William Hoover's vacuum cleaners all capitalized on the ability to mass produce products and distribute via large-scale retail organizations such as Sears.

After the Second World War, the global demand for new ideas within an increasingly consumer-focused society provided the pull, and emerging new technologies provided the push for a wealth of new and exciting ideas. Demand for products as diverse as sports cars, roller-blades, personal computers, and mobile phones, together with a business enthusiasm to benefit from their delivery, have accelerated the uptake of new ideas. It is particularly in the past 30 years that the ability of more and more individuals and organizations to gain from taking ideas to market has become more evident. As technology has developed at an ever more rapid pace, new markets have developed and existing markets have themselves evolved, the opportunities available from the successful exploitation of new ideas have grown significantly. Multinationals have spread their influence and at the same time smaller companies have become more able to extend their reach outside traditional domestic market-places and, in doing so, organizations of all types have embraced new approaches to help them improve the effectiveness of their idea creation, selection, and delivery capabilities. This recent evolution of what can be seen as a developing innovation capability has occurred in three core phases.

PHASE 1 – PUTTING THE BASICS IN PLACE

The first major period of recent advance in how organizations have taken ideas to market occurred in the early to mid-1980s, when companies facing the challenges of increased competition and more rapid technological advancement sought to accommodate several new issues. At the forefront of this was the increasing role of technology in new products and services. From semi-conductors to composite materials, database management software to call centers, the adoption of new technology became a core strategic focus for many companies and, as a means to effecting this, the management of external alliances to facilitate the transfer of the appropriate technologies from lead innovators, universities, and other research establishments became a key challenge.

Understanding the technology, never mind selecting the most appropriate for the application, was a major headache for many. Furthermore, ensuring that access, integration, upgrading, and support were managed in a coherent and focused manner was, in many cases, a black art. At the same time, although largely focused on their regional markets, companies were increasingly aware of issues such as quality and reliability. The advances being made by Toyota and others in the automotive industry were having widespread impact as more organizations adopted the "total quality" mantra in their bid to improve idea delivery and support. In addition, as growth generated from new products and services became ever more important, many organizations began to create dedicated resources focused on idea creation, selection, and delivery. To support this, they also began to introduce recently created improvements such as stage-gated development processes. Together, this combination of focused resources and defined processes helped to deliver significant improvements in the efficiency of taking ideas to market, but there were still a number of further advances to be made.

PHASE 2 – GLOBALIZATION AND ACCELERATION

With the fundamental elements of access to technology and dedicated resources in place, all focused on creating and delivering ideas into their local market-places, the next step forward for many leading organizations occurred in the decade between 1985 and 1995. As globalization simultaneously opened new markets and increased the sources of competition, several key advances in approach were implemented. From a market perspective, the ability and the need to embrace a worldwide market-place meant that the focus for idea delivery had to change. Rather than address just their local needs, organizations had to accommodate a wider diversity of end product and service requirements that differed from area to area. At the same time they had to ensure that sufficient commonality was present in the delivery and support of their products and services to benefit economically from scale.

Examples of how companies tackled this dichotomy include the use of common automotive platforms across multiple markets but with local customization to regional needs – GM, Buick, Cadillac, and Chevrolet in the US; Opel in Germany; Isuzu in Japan; Vauxhall in the UK; and Saab in Sweden – and a similar effect in the consumer electronics industry with shared components for multiple products – Philips for European and US mid-range, Grundig for European high-end, and Marantz for Japanese mass market audio equipment.

Allied to this commonality was the increasingly important role of the brand in communicating and supporting new ideas. Whether this was in the form of multiple brands applied to common products or, as in the case of Nike, the extension of a single brand across multiple global product ranges; or, as with the Coca-Cola Company and Procter & Gamble, how to use a common brand across products, each of which were customized to local tastes and consumer behaviors; or, as with Intel and Nutrasweet, the introduction of ingredient branding; the increasing significance of the brand in the delivery of new ideas became core.

In parallel with this, in order to create and deliver the best new products and services it became doubly necessary to focus both on doing the right things and on doing them quickly. This led to organizations trying to focus more on their core competencies (power transmissions for Honda, optics and electronics for Canon, printing for Hewlett Packard) and at the same time accelerate their idea delivery. This correspondingly facilitated the introduction of fuzzy-gate development processes to speed up decision-making, multi-disciplinary teams to engage all functions simultaneously, increased involvement of suppliers to reduce cost and complexity, and matrix organizational structures to accommodate the team/functional alignments and allegiance. All of these were elements of a more complex corporate capability that was quickly becoming a key differentiator in the market-place between winners and losers.

PHASE 3 – FOCUS AND INTEGRATION

The third major phase in the evolution of organizations' capability to deliver competitive, value-adding, and sustainable new ideas came into place in the final few years of the twentieth century. As the ability to use flexible supply chains, global branding and cross-cultural teams became the norm for many organizations, the two key differentiators that came into play in this were focus and integration. Focus, in terms of the customer and how to deliver an idea. Integration, in terms of sharing information, skills, technologies, and effort.

Differentiation for the end user has become a key issue because global products and services are now commonplace: BodyShop, GAP, and Hennes & Mauritz on every major high street and in every mall; Hyatts and Sheratons provide the same menu to identical rooms, all with the same soaps and bed linen; and CNN, Discovery Channel, and HBO are available from every cable operator. Ensuring that customers perceive a tailored service or personalized product has driven the concepts of mass customization of niche products using common platforms and modular components across sectors, from Dell to Mercedes to Amanpuri resorts and Banyan Tree boutique hotels.

The economies of scale are still there but, to the consumer, there is an impression of individuality and focus on satisfying their specific requirements.

Enabling such new products and services to be delivered on a global scale and still produce profit has demanded a previously unimaginable level of co-operation and integration between organizations. Not only are companies choosing to work more closely with all stakeholders, from suppliers, distributors, and retailers to customers, investors, and critics, but they are also working in partnership with competitors. In contrast to the great video débâcle between Betamax and VHS, DVD products are now being developed through co-operation between Sony, Toshiba, Matsushita, Philips *et al.*; VirginMoney.com has been developed in co-operation between the Royal Bank of Scotland and Australia's AMP; EPOC, the PDA operating system, is owned by Symbian, a joint venture between Psion, Ericsson, Panasonic, Motorola, and Nokia; and Bluetooth, the new wireless applications standard, has over 200 companies involved in its development and exploitation. Companies recognize that, in many areas, only by working together to establish new global standards can they individually create the environment in which their new ideas can be successful. As a consequence, there has been increased integration of R&D activities and more firms are becoming part of inter-disciplinary networks.

EMERGING ISSUES

Today, as the innovation leaders strive to make the next step in the evolution of this increasingly fast, diverse, and complex arena, there is a whole new set of issues coming onto the horizon for many firms. Like total quality management, ingredient branding, and mass customization, some of these are being developed in one sector and will transfer across sectors in the next few years, whilst others are more generic in application from the start.

» Companies like 3M are now looking for increasing opportunities for cross-business exploitation of new technologies and the associated re-use of their intellectual capital.

» With the advance of the Internet as a sales and distribution channel, mass customization of products is evolving into tailored services unique to the individual with mySAP, myNetscape, and myeBay all becoming established for personal content and service delivery.

» The increasing convergence of new technologies, especially mobile communications and PCs is driving companies such as IBM, Dell, Motorola, Microsoft, and Nokia to share development and also the underpinning intellectual property rights.

» Industries from advertising and media to software and catering are increasingly using temporary expert groups of freelance professionals to create, develop, and even deliver new products and services.

Together, these and other, as yet embryonic, issues, are ensuring that the way in which individuals, companies, and governments deliver new ideas to the market will continue to evolve at an ever more rapid pace.

KEY LEARNING POINTS

» Innovation exploded in the seventeenth century, in part because of conditions that allowed cross-functional, multi-disciplinary discussion.

» The early twentieth century saw the arrival of mass production together with the large-scale retail distribution organization necessary to bring mass-produced goods to market.

» The early to mid-1980s was marked by the increased importance of technologically driven innovation. Simultaneously, interest in issues such as quality and reliability reached a peak.

» 1985 to 1995 was the decade of globalization with an emphasis on global scale, global brand power, a focus on core competencies and partnering for effective supply-chain management.

» The final few years of the twentieth century were characterized by an emphasis on customer focus, mass customization, and integration of knowledge, technology, and information within and across organizations.

» The early years of the twenty-first century are seeing further development of mass-customized, tailored services. Additionally, organizational forms are changing as companies seek to leverage skills and knowledge and to source innovation increasingly from *ad hoc*, freelance teams of experts.

The E-Dimension

How has the Internet enabled and restricted how ideas are exploited? How important has the technology side of the equation been in creating and delivering value? This chapter reviews the impact of the Internet on taking ideas to market by:

- » questioning the real competitive advantage that has been gained;
- » examining eBay as a phenomenal success story of the first Internet age;
- » looking at the increasingly difficult issue of satisfying customer expectations; and
- » providing an example of the use of Internet technology to enhance innovation.

The Art of War, written by Sun Tzu in 300BC, is a manual for warfare still used in the twenty-first century by generals and business leaders alike. But for all his wisdom on leadership and tactics, Sun Tzu does not once mention the use of technological innovation for winning wars. During the last century technology created many victories. It also led to a Cold War in which both sides escalated spending, yet could not gain strategic advantage. Many CEOs and dot.com executives will recognize that feeling: non-proprietary technology rarely creates long-term competitive benefits.

The Internet tends to level the commercial battlefield and this means that innovative capability will become increasingly important for generating superior shareholder returns. Competitive advantage will increasingly be found by using Internet technologies creatively to gain short-lived, temporary monopolies.

THE INTERNET AND COMPETITIVE ADVANTAGE

For a brief period, the Internet challenged the established economic order. The "New Economy" unleashed a set of unprecedented stock market valuations for firms like Amazon.com, eBay, and lastminute.com. The market's optimism was based on a set of beliefs in escalating productivity gains driven by IT, hyper-growth in online consumer demand, and exponential first-mover advantage for the Web pioneers. Not many of these new economy articles of faith have remained intact.

However, despite the bursting of the dot.com bubble, as the Internet matures it will continue to disrupt established industries, to sharpen the competitive pressure on undifferentiated offerings, and to drive innovation. It is both a global operating system for generating ideas and a ruthless commoditizer of profit.

There is a precedent for all of this in the history of the electricity industry. During the 1880s, US manufacturers introduced electricity to their factories. Surprisingly, this led neither to rapid productivity gains nor to any substantial advantage for the first movers in this new technology. In fact, the introduction of electric power depressed profits in US manufacturing for three decades and created no appreciable productivity gains until around 1915.

The winners were not the first movers, but the clever movers. Those who simply wired up their old steam age factories succeeded only in adding a layer of cost. The real significance of electricity was that, for the first time, machines could be remote from their power supplies, a precondition for innovations like cell layout and flexible manufacturing systems in modern production. The winners, at least temporarily, were the businesses that used electricity to innovate; manufacturing process innovation was everything, technology was merely an enabler. So has history repeated itself in today's IT revolution? In many ways, it has.

The last decade saw unprecedented capital expenditure on IT, as blue chip corporates and dot.coms alike sought to gain competitive advantage through ERP, CRM, BPR, Web-enablement, and a host of other technologies. This investment has almost certainly contributed to a rise in US productivity in the latter half of the 1990s, but there is a paradox in this growth. Average operating margins for large US companies have stayed virtually static for the entire decade at around 15%; it's as if the world's companies had been running ever harder up a down escalator just to stay still. The likelihood is that those hard-won productivity gains have gone mainly to consumers not producers.

To create superior shareholder returns, technology is necessary, but not sufficient. Efficient, e-enabled processes are likely to become a hygiene factor where any element of price sensitivity exists, but real competitive advantage cannot be bought from an IT company that sells the same product to each of your competitors. It may, however, come from learning to use the technology in innovative ways that in turn create genuine advantage. Perhaps the greatest example of this is eBay.

EBAY CASE STUDY

"Disappears faster than a dot.com company," proclaimed a recent advert for Hyundai cars. Unlike many of its fellow dot.coms, eBay will not be disappearing any time soon. The story goes that Pierre Omidyar founded eBay as an online auction site when his girlfriend was collecting Pez sweet bottles. How did eBay grow from swapping childrens' sweet containers into a company with ten times the value of Sotheby's in seven years?

The eureka moment was when Omidyar noticed that his girlfriend suffered from a lack of "market liquidity" in the pursuit of her hobby. Collectables – the kind of stuff that gets traded in car boot sales and market squares all over the world – are bought and sold avidly, but the trick to buying is to be in the right place at the right time. This, of course, is easier said than done – to succeed, I need to know what seller, in what market, in what town, in what country, on what day, will have the right object at the right price. All over the world, second-hand dealers make money by exploiting this problem. By knowing their markets better than anyone else they profit from customers' imperfect knowledge and the high cost to consumers of searching for products.

Omidyar saw how Internet technology could cut through these market imperfections by creating what amounts to a 24-hour, global car boot sale. Sellers initiate an auction by posting a description of the product onto the eBay Website. Buyers use the company's software to make bids, and to complete a transaction the seller and winning bidder simply negotiate payment and shipping details between themselves. eBay provides copious advice on how to do this, but does not act as an intermediary.

eBay's users transacted $2.25bn of gross merchandise sales in the first half of 2001 and eBay itself made $148mn gross profit on net revenues of just $170mn – a gross profit margin in excess of 80%. Even taking into account costs like marketing and IT, net profit margins are 20% compared to an average of 15% for the largely mature businesses of the S&P 500. It is one of the few dot.com companies that has been robustly profitable, almost from the start. What explains eBay's success?

The answer includes equal measures of luck and judgment. Omidyar's understanding of the Internet's potential was truly ahead of its time and was rooted not in technology *per se*, but in an observation of a genuine, unmet consumer need. In 1993, when eBay was founded, Internet commerce had only just been permitted by the Internet standards governing body, the Internet browser had been invented one year previously and public debate was about whether the Internet would ever be used by anyone except technology geeks. At such an early stage, it required a genuine leap of imagination and a willingness to take risk to create a new business.

eBay was able to translate this early insight into genuine first-mover advantage. First-mover advantage has been one of the shibboleths of the dot.com era – usually meaning little in practice other than an ability to burn cash quickly on expensive marketing and non-proprietary technology. eBay gained genuine advantage by being the first online market-place to gain scale. If I want to sell goods, I will much prefer taking them to a market with 100 buyers instead of just one. Similarly, if I'm buying, I prefer a market where there are lots of people selling. This simple truth creates a virtuous circle for eBay – the more people who use it, the more valuable it becomes to each of its users and the harder it becomes for a competitor to challenge it. eBay reinforces this virtuous circle by allowing buyers to review sellers to provide the element of trust that can be missing when sales are not conducted face to face.

eBay will have to sustain its growth to maintain its share price and the true test of a company's innovative capacity is whether it can keep inventing beyond its first idea. For eBay, there are three strands to that strategy – expanding into new territories, new markets, and new products. Fortune has smiled upon eBay in the pursuit of its first goal. The dot.com crash has enabled it to move quickly into new countries by buying up local companies that had copied its business model but were subsequently forced to sell at fire-sale prices. The company is also seeking to move away from its original consumer-to-consumer model by leveraging its technology to provide virtual storefronts for SMEs. Perhaps most difficult of all, the company has entered the second-hand car market through its partnership with AutoTrader, a used car dealership.

Time will tell how successful these business extensions will be, but eBay stands as a great example of a company that was first to understand how new technology could meet an old human need.

THE INTERNET AND CONSUMERS

According to *Creative Good* (2000), 62% of online shoppers have given up purchasing a service or product online at least once due to inadequate search or navigational mechanisms, invisible product ranges or Flash plug-ins and downloads. Customers expect not only speed and accuracy on the Internet, but also to be able to complete their purchase online in a way that is usable, functional, and corresponds with their needs.

The Internet provides its consumers with more choice and more information – this in turn leads to a more competitive environment in which a company has to succeed by providing the right service in the right way to its consumers. The Internet differs from the traditional bricks-and-mortar market-place, in that customers are more fickle and the cost for switching suppliers is minimal, if not non-existent. Creating brand loyalty and Web-stickiness can only be achieved through providing a service that is compelling at every stage, from the proposition to the fulfillment.

Boo.com, the infamous Web-failure, started with a bright idea and an enticing proposition combined with extensive news coverage and advertisement; Boo created an idea of being able to provide the latest and trendiest sports clothes for urban, wealthy individuals. The technology however was, quite literally, not up to speed. The Boo.com Website was buggy, and took too long for customers to download. In addition, the service was only enabled on PCs – something that was rather unfortunate, as Boo discovered when launching in France. At the time, the majority of French computers were Apple Macs. Ultimately, Boo.com failed to offer an engaging customer experience, failed to retain its customers and therefore, eventually, failed to stay in business.

Today's online services are more and more created from a customer-centric perspective. Through creating an engaging and compelling customer experience, companies will be able to attract and retain customers, increase customer spend, and reduce operating costs, as customers migrate from more expensive channels, such as call centers and branches.

The design of online services has developed from something that was initiated and developed in-house, and finally tested focusing on pure usability before going live, to being a process that involves the customer throughout. What creates an engaging customer experience is a service that is not only usable, but also something that responds to what the customers want, in a way that suits them. Thus, the customers are continuously involved in both proposition development stage and the user interface design phase. Designers, developers, and marketers hold a continuous dialogue with the customer by using a range of online and offline techniques and tools that allow them to assess customers' responses and attitudes, as well as actual usage of the proposition under development.

The process of designing an online service encompasses a wide range of resources, both internal and external – design, legal, marketing, technical, and operations. Not all of these skills are necessarily found in one organization and, as a consequence, the development process has become one of integrating skills and expertise and building a network of skill domains.

THE CHANGING TECHNOLOGY

In addition to enabling customers to purchase services and products online, according to Forrester Research, the Internet research company, the Internet has become even more significant as a tool for pre-purchase research. Jack Nasser (CEO of Ford Motors) recently said that no one in the US buys a car any more without first looking on the Internet. Consequently, dealers are faced with customers who know as much about automobiles' price and features as they do.

In a sense, this is moving us towards the economists' model of a perfect market. Picture a row of stalls all selling potatoes. All the stallholders are offering an identical product, the customer knows everything about potato prices, and it takes little or no effort to compare each stall. In this world everybody is beaten down to an average, low level of profitability. Something similar is happening in some parts of the retail financial industry. In the nascent online sharebroking industry of 1995, Ameritrade commanded a price of almost \$32 per trade and e*Trade charged \$24 per transaction. But just four years later prices had fallen to \$14 and \$10 respectively.

One implication of a world of more frictionless capitalism is that making average products competently, even with a good brand, is unlikely to continue to generate superior shareholder value. Companies will have to continue to succeed in providing over and above customer expectations, using the latest technology at competitive prices.

To do this, some companies will focus on being price leaders, generating profits by maintaining a low cost-base through e-enabled processes, hyper-efficient partnering, and ruthless cost control. Others will use the Internet to provide greater value to customers through enhanced convenience or greater personalization. A very large group will focus on using intranets and other technologies to leverage their intellectual capital.

In the last few hundred years, the arts of war, commerce, and creativity have been profoundly affected by technology. As the dust of the dot.com bust settles, a new, more mature, attitude to technology-driven innovation and product development has emerged. To ignore the profound impact of new technology would be foolish in the extreme. After all, Sun Tzu's tactics alone would not defeat a modern army.

BEST PRACTICE: USING INTERNET TECHNOLOGY TO STIMULATE INNOVATION

A global top-50 asset management company with major presence in Europe and Asia-Pacific responded to the stock market crash and subsequent bear market of the year 2000 with an emphasis on developing new product ideas and driving up business efficiency. Recessionary times had made equity investments less attractive to individuals and institutions alike and many investors were choosing to keep a greater percentage of their portfolios in cash – directly harming the group's revenues.

Although the group was historically strong in a number of specialist sectors and regions, it was not innovating to the same extent as competitors, many of which had rolled out new products like themed investments or hedge funds that promised investors absolute returns whether the market rose or fell.

The group had previously invested in a global intranet for its employees to share knowledge and one senior manager in the company lobbied hard to develop an application for the Web that would allow employees to submit and jointly develop ideas for new products and business efficiencies.

Previous innovation initiatives had achieved mixed results, often duplicating existing ideas, or simply failing to produce anything of significant value. Nonetheless, the most senior managers in the company regarded innovation as a top priority and backed the development of an intranet bulletin board to facilitate product development. To assist this process, the company appointed a number of executives to work with the originators of ideas placed on the Web.

Previously, employees suggesting ideas were given a *pro forma* letter informing that their idea had been received and was being considered by the appropriate executives. Eventually a substantive response would be sent that amounted to little more than a "yes" or "no." Under the new system, one of the facilitating executives, who themselves were relatively senior, would contact the originator, personally, by phone. Their brief was to help the originator fully articulate the idea, and to channel it on to the next stage of development. But the contact itself served to value people in a way that the old bureaucratic "thank you for your suggestion" memos did not.

Another benefit of the product development bulletin board was that employees could contribute "half-an-idea" and allow other employees to discuss and develop it. This related to the issue of a "development gap" in the company's business processes. The company had found that asking for ideas produced too many responses of little value that flooded its selection system, whereas asking for fully formed business cases produced too few contributions. The intranet system provided a way of building embryonic product ideas into full-scale propositions.

The company also found that it had to work hard on the culture and behavior that surrounded the innovation process. Professional skepticism and rigorous evidence-based enquiry can handicap the generation and early stage development of ideas. To overcome these issues, the company trained a number of its executives in creativity and idea facilitation skills. It also provided employees with a reason to be motivated to produce new ideas by offering a cash prize of around $80,000 for any substantial ideas reaching implementation, together with a number of smaller rewards for completing each different stage of idea development.

The result of the intranet ideas bulletin board has been the creation of two new and profitable product lines for the group within eight months. From an ideas pipeline of close to zero before implementation, there are now 26 distinct product ideas and enhancements that the company is actively pursuing.

The key learning points have been that, although technology can stimulate a company's imagination capital, you have to work hard to get those benefits. Even intranet technology cannot make ideas "just happen." Processes must be built that are both quick and non-bureaucratic and also sufficiently robust to support creativity in a large company. Technology is also no substitute for getting the people issues right. This means that people need to encounter not just the right reward and recognition at the end of the process, but also the right positive, development-orientated behaviors when they suggest ideas initially.

KEY LEARNING POINTS

» Non-proprietary technology rarely creates long-term competitive advantage or, except in very limited cases, any substantial first-mover advantage.

» The Internet tends to commoditize product and service offerings by lowering search and switching costs and by imposing standardized forms of comparison across product categories.

» However, companies can generate competitive advantage by learning to use technology to provide innovative and compelling customer propositions.

» Consequently, the design of online services is becoming intensely customer focused at all stages – involving a continuous dialogue with the customer from proposition design through to usability testing.

» Internet technology can also be used inside a company to facilitate the generation and development of ideas.

The Global Dimension

What are the impacts of globalization on innovation and idea exploitation? This chapter addresses some of the issues and provides insights into some of the implications, including:

» delivering new products and services into a global market-place;
» organizations in the new global arena;
» enabling the individual to operate successfully in a global environment; and
» how ABB redefined itself to successfully compete on the world stage.

The history of globalization has been acted out in two parts. The "old globalization" of the 1970s and 1980s was about making products in a central location and selling them worldwide without distinction. The problem was that the complexity of national preferences and cultures counted for a lot more to the average buyer than global scale economics.

The "new globalization," which was born in the 90s, is about creating a web of value through the best possible configuration of local and global markets, locations, products, people, and processes. The "new globalization" presents complexity and opportunity for taking ideas to market. The fundamental building blocks for getting it right are an understanding of global product strategy, global location, and global people.

Ask anyone to name a global product and the chances are they will say either McDonald's or Coca-Cola. But truly global products like the Big Mac are the exception not the rule. "Even underwear has local characteristics," says John H. Bryan of the Sara-Lee Corporation (an American multinational).

Global product strategy tends to be a question of degree rather than a "yes/no" decision. In the automotive industry, European drivers prefer smaller cars with hard suspension, an emphasis on fuel economy and a gray or black interior finish. A classic American Buick or Cadillac with its low fuel efficiency, large turning circle, soft suspension, and color-coordinated interior is not a winning proposition for the average European driver. Similarly, few Americans would want to drive a Fiat. But these obvious differences have not prevented automobile manufacturers from successfully globalizing many of the components of their cars. For example the Ford Lincoln in America looks very different to the European Jaguar S Type and Volvo S40 and yet shares the same platform. Given that chassis development can account for up to one-third of the cost of manufacture, it's not surprising that many manufacturers have found substantial economies through standardizing components.

GLOBAL PRODUCT INNOVATION

The search for efficiencies is one of the biggest drivers of global product innovation, especially in industries with high product development costs. The higher these costs, the more sense it makes to focus globally on selling higher volumes of fewer products, rather than tailoring product development to individual local markets. This raises severe challenges to companies that are organized on a national basis. Prior to its rationalization, Black & Decker (a US power tools company) had a structure in which country managers made decisions on product design and development. Unsurprisingly, "not invented here" syndrome led the company to produce over 100 different types of motor worldwide, with all the attendant cost, complexity, and duplication – something that its rivals, Bosch and Makita, avoided.

To avoid "not invented here," organizations need a global product view that in turn requires some degree of global product management. However, this only makes sense when customers have needs that transcend national boundaries. Notwithstanding differences in national health care systems and epidemiology, disease strikes the world's citizens in a similar way everywhere – a coronary attack is a coronary attack, wherever it happens. Thus, drugs like Prozac and Viagra speak to universally felt needs that are experienced in the same way everywhere. Contrast this with a US kitchen equipment manufacturer trying to enter the Japanese market. On average, kitchens in Japan are 60% smaller than in America. A refrigerator designed for the US market is simply not going to fit a Japanese kitchen.

Customer understanding is one of the building blocks of great product development and many products have a high local cultural content. Unfortunately, this means that trade-offs between local customization and global product development are inevitable. When Canon, the Japanese electronics giant, decided to go into photocopiers in the 1970s, it started from scratch to design a global product. However, its home market in Japan has a range of paper sizes that are not used in the rest of the world. Canon decided not to support all Japanese formats, thus trading-off the ability to fully satisfy its domestic customers for a simpler, cheaper component platform that could be leveraged globally. Good product design needs to begin with an understanding of any product's global and local market aspirations.

However, even when that aspiration is clear, there are many examples of failed moves into new markets. At a product level, failures often happen because global manufacturers are not close enough to local customers to respond to changes in taste. Benetton, the retail fashion group, overcomes this difficulty through the design of its supply chain. The group manufactures in Italy and sells in most parts of the world in an industry that is highly fragmented by local tastes and culture. Most manufacturers make woolen clothes from pre-colored yarns, but Benetton makes them *in greggio* (in gray) and only adds color "just in time" to meet emerging demand in each of its local markets. Although this is a slightly more expensive manufacturing process, it allows Benetton to respond rapidly to changing needs in any of its local markets whilst keeping most of the scale benefits of focused global manufacturing.

ORGANIZATIONS IN THE NEW GLOBAL ARENA

So what should marketers, strategists, and product designers faced with global issues be considering? The first question is whether your products really do have global potential. Consider the following.

» Are my customers global (other multinational corporations, for example) or do they have common needs that transcend national boundaries?
» Are my product development costs so high that I need to amortize them across as many markets as possible?
» Are my competitors global companies or foreign entrants?
» How significant and varied are local product preferences and how can I achieve the least possible trade-off between global scale and local customization?
» What elements of the product can be sourced or manufactured on a global basis?

Assuming that the answer to at least some of these questions is "yes," the next obvious question that a global approach to product development raises is "where?" The "old" style of globalization had an easy answer to this – take a local product and sell everywhere you can. "New" globalization tends to look at both the sales and supply side of the value chain.

On the sales side, country selection is about understanding which national markets offer the best fit with a firm's core competencies (its brand, knowledge, product, processes, people, and other strategic assets) together with the greatest market potential and lowest barriers to entry. Of course, there is often a trade-off between each of these dynamics, and it is generally better to make strategic choices on a regional or global basis, than to pick off one stand-alone country at a time.

On the supply side, access to technology and knowledge has become an ever more important driver of decision-making. There is nothing new in locating product design and manufacture in countries that offer the best access to skills, technology, and manufacturing resources. Indeed, modern economic observations suggest that local, highly specific industry "clusters" are a major determinant of competitiveness. "Clusters" are defined as local areas that create a unique area of capability that is unequalled in the rest of the world. In his book *The Competitive Advantage of Nations*, Porter wrote about the Italian tile cluster that occupies an area within a six-mile radius of the village of Sassuolo in Northern Italy. Other examples of clusters include the City of London for financial services and Silicon Valley for digital technology. The paradox of global product design is that it may require very fine local knowledge and precise location to truly deliver great products with global potential.

However, a pitfall of the "cluster" approach to innovation is that it has the potential to ghettoize creativity and to disenfranchise the creativity of employees who are not in the "innovation hub." Ultimately this is a people issue and a successful global approach to product design is not possible without the global people policies to match.

Wal-Mart, the great American retailer, holds an annual employee convention. The Wal-Mart corporate song is a traditional feature of the convention and binds its American workforce: "Who's the greatest? W . . . A . . . L – M . . . A . . . R . . . T." Employees swivel their hips after the "L" to indicate the hyphen. Wal-Mart's German employees in Europe are said to prefer to hide in the toilets than to sing along. National difference counts for a lot.

Ultimately, no company can be truly transnational without changing mindsets, but even when possible this can be costly and time-consuming. However, even without engaging in major organizational change, product developers with a global view need to think about the effects of leadership, organization and cultural issues on their ability to succeed.

Most companies have an administrative heritage that is nationally biased. Business units are frequently structured along national boundaries, jealousies exist between home market nationals and other employees, and national boundaries and preferences prevail. In practice this reduces the ability to share ideas, knowledge, processes, and product components across national boundaries.

Organization also has a fundamental role in enabling a global approach. Business units have evolved more often than not with a national purpose in mind. Often their MDs and senior teams are rewarded on national, not global performance. Business unit organization raises two fundamental questions – how to ensure that business units co-operate globally and how to ensure that their commitment to today's successful products does not inhibit the development of future ideas.

A common solution to the problem of global collaboration has been to put in place a matrix structure, in which managers have both global product responsibility and national segment responsibilities. The advantage, at least in theory, of this approach is to keep local market focus whilst maximizing global earnings. In practice, managers commonly report exhaustion and paralysis as product managers, country managers and functional managers attempt to negotiate their often conflicting priorities.

Alternative approaches to organization are beginning to emerge. A major European mobile phone company is currently considering dispensing entirely with traditional business units as it strives to innovate quickly on a global basis. Instead the company is seeking to organize itself around the product development life cycle. One business unit holds global responsibility for vision, ideas, and new product development. A second concentrates on marketing expertise to bring the idea to market as quickly as possible and the third concentrates on organizational excellence in delivery of established services.

THE GLOBAL APPROACH TO PEOPLE WITHIN

A global approach to product development also requires a global approach to people. Here the issues are about the integration of home and foreign market nationals, the management of diversity, and team dynamics. Many multinationals have an expatriate management culture in which executives take the majority of top jobs in local markets from the home market. This colonial management style makes for efficiency but creates problems in the war for local talent. Why should ambitious, highly skilled local talent work for a company with a glass ceiling based on nationality? Instead, high-potential product developers, marketers, and managers need to gain experience in all the company's strategically important markets. IBM, for example, implemented a policy in its international division that no executive could be promoted beyond a certain level unless they had completed a foreign assignment. This approach has since been emulated by 3M in its Global Product/Local Execution initiative.

This approach inevitably raises the issue of global teaming. At best, diverse, global teams design better and more innovative solutions because they have a richer range of knowledge, experience and perspective to draw on. At worst, global teams are modern management's Tower of Babel – creativity and efficiency can crumble in the face of national difference, stereotype, and misunderstanding.

Getting the best out of a multinational team requires excellent facilitation and some cultural sensitivity. During his research at IBM, Geert Hofstede, the Dutch academic, developed a tool for understanding national cultures based on a series of dimensions. For example, the US and many European countries emphasize individualism – identity is based on the individual, leadership is the ideal and individual achievement is respected. By contrast, Japan and China tend to be collective in attitude – identity is based on the social system, and membership of a group a powerful basis of respect. Understanding these differences is key to getting teams to perform. For example, US- and European-style individual appraisals tend to be perceived as threatening in cultures with a collectivist norm.

Whatever the realities of national difference, perception and stereotype can often inhibit multinational product development. These perception distances are very real. For example, research by Cranfield School of Management found that Italian and Spanish managers view the British as highly educated but not very competent, whereas British managers see themselves as more competent than average.

Similarly, French managers are regarded by other Europeans as lacking compassion, and Spanish professionals are generally perceived negatively across a range of dimensions. These perception gaps can lead to intuitive decisions and behaviors within teams that are wrong. It requires facilitation to get the most out of a team of people that do not have experience of working across national boundaries.

Globalization in product development is interconnected with questions of organizational form and global people management. Fierce, global competition means that all but the most exceptional product innovations are unlikely to confer more than a year or two's competitive advantage. A major process improvement may give three to five years' relative advantage before competitors copy it. The most enduring source of advantage, however, is likely to be organizational transformation that enables companies to be locally responsive and globally competitive. ABB's vision of becoming "multi-domestic" is the standard-bearer for this approach.

BEST PRACTICE: ASEA BROWN BOVERI (ABB) – EQUIPPING FOR GLOBAL COMPETITION

When Percy Barnevik became CEO of ABB in 1983 he found a challenge. The Swedish/Swiss engineering company had an export-orientated, technocratic culture that many regarded as over-centralized and bureaucratic. The company's business units operated as national fiefdoms with great local autonomy but little global co-ordination. The company faced excess capacity, weakened demand, and increased competition from global competitors.

Barnevik introduced a two-stage strategy focused on restructuring and then global growth. Restructuring was initially drastic. Barnevik retained only 10% of corporate HQ staff; the remainder went either to operating companies, projects, or redundancy. A new global matrix structure gave managers responsibility both for local markets and global products. This allowed global co-ordination at ABB for the first time, and was backed up by a number of other changes.

Barnevik's personal schedule was grueling as he traveled the world to communicate the changes – he estimates that he spent

80% of his time traveling and presented 5000 PowerPoint slides during a single year. This was accompanied by a new corporate identity and a policy that made English the official corporate language.

The role of country managers was to articulate customer-focused, local market strategies whilst global product managers' task was to develop and champion worldwide strategies to capitalize on economies of scale and co-ordinate and approve R&D and product development around the world.

Another part of the glue that held this matrix together was ABACUS, ABB's new management information system. ABACUS tracked 32 performance measures across 5000 profit centers and compared the variance between budget forecasts and actuals. Most importantly it allowed data to be broken down by both global product line or business segment and country or company.

During the mid-1990s, ABB moved its matrix towards a regional focus on three trading blocs – Europe, the Americas, and Asia. In part, this was a response to the growing importance of large projects within ABB that were neither country- nor product-specific.

As a result of these changes, ABB was voted "Europe's most respected company" and has been described as the "post-multi-national company of the future." Nonetheless, by the late 1990s further issues became apparent. ABB's customers were predominantly global corporations and so regional boundaries were diluting. The industry as a whole continued to be highly competitive and the "multi-domestic" focus made it more difficult to capture scale economies than for competitors with focused product development and manufacture in single locations. The matrix structure also led to exhaustion and conflict between staff.

ABB responded by splitting itself into smaller segments and abandoning its regional structures. Segments and business areas now took global responsibility with country managers reporting directly into the group. Additionally, ABB is moving away from its engineering heritage towards a more knowledge- and service-orientated culture. This has placed a much greater emphasis on developing technology and managing global leadership and human capital.

KEY LEARNING POINTS

» The "old globalization" of 1970s and 1980s was about selling in as many markets as possible. By contrast, the "new globalization" of the 1990s seeks to create a web of value through the optimal configuration of local and global markets, people, products, and processes.

» Very few completely global products, such as the "Big Mac," exist but many products are based around a core, global platform that is tailored for each local market.

» Products with relatively high development costs are particularly susceptible to globalization, as are those with global customers.

» Creating global products generally requires trade-offs between global scale economies and exactly meeting locally specific needs.

» Successful global product strategy also requires a global approach to people and organization that includes matrix structures to co-ordinate product development and facilitation, and cultural awareness to support multinational teams.

The State of the Art

What is state of the art for innovation right now? This chapter navigates through the maze of current issues to highlight the key emerging themes by:

- » providing a contextual understanding of the evolutionary position of firms;
- » discussing the key drivers of change;
- » identifying how organizations are responding to the challenges they encounter; and
- » questioning what is next.

CONTEXT

State of the art in taking ideas to market depends on where an individual, a company, or even an industrial sector is in the overall context of the evolution of innovation capability. As detailed in Chapter 3, following an increasing build-up during the first three-quarters of the twentieth century, it is only in the past 20 years that there have been significant, or even revolutionary, changes in how ideas are being taken to market. Some companies have adapted the latest thinking coming out of the academic establishment, learnt from other sectors in the business community, and are now even beginning to operate at what can be considered to be the leading edge. Some are integrating approaches such as stage-gate processes and multi-functional teams, as it has become apparent to them that others have gained from their adoption. By contrast, other firms are only now just beginning to take the first step and start to grasp the basics, aligning their desire to exploit new technologies with the concept of a coherent strategy, flexible process, and dedicated resource. Ironically, some organizations that, by the nature of the technological changes that they are seeking to exploit, feel they are at the cutting edge are, in reality, just getting off the starting blocks.

State of the art is something that is clearly contextual and therefore something that, for some, may well be process-driven but, for others, can be more a matter of strategy. However, given the critical and mutual dependency between process, strategy, and organization in the ability to deliver new products and services, perhaps the most fundamental changes that are occurring across sectors are in the organization. As process and strategy have arguably evolved at a higher rate, it is now the ways in which companies are structuring themselves, their suppliers, and their partners that is the main issue. State of the art today can be seen to be largely linked to the core organizational aspects of innovation and it is attention here that is enabling firms to improve their innovation performance, generate better ideas, and create value from their delivery. The Bauhaus movement famously declared that "form follows function." Each of the changes in this chapter is about organizational form following an ever-greater pursuit of innovation.

Between 1965 and 1979 the number of workers involved in employee suggestion schemes in the German Democratic Republic rose from

600,000 to 1.7 million. An interest in innovation and product development is not the sole preserve of capitalism. Paradoxically, modern companies exhibit a number of features that are Soviet-like in appearance. Think of central planning, capital rationing, and the muted link between individuals' value contribution and their remuneration.

Socialist East German goods and services would have flooded the world market if worker suggestion schemes had been sufficient to create innovation. But as surely as economic decay and a desire for freedom hastened the collapse of socialism, so too will market forces continue to create changes in Western companies.

DRIVERS OF CHANGE

The greatest drivers of this change, today as in the past half-century, are technology, competition, and shifts in attitude. Largely as a result of technology and social change, material prosperity in developed countries has risen more in the past 50 years than in the previous 10,000. Successive waves of disruptive technology have begun to beat on the commercial shoreline with ever-greater intensity and rapidity. Digital technologies like the Internet, mobile telephony, and related wireless services change commercial realities at breakneck speed. For example, in just 60 years the price of a long distance telephone call from the US went from almost $100 per minute to less than 10 cents. Biotechnology, wireless, and nano-technology are sunrise industries. Whether or not they create long-term value for their shareholders, these industries will, in a short space of time, create entirely new propositions, possibilities, and economic realities. These technological waves will impact many sectors, and the challenge for many companies is to respond quickly enough to survive and thrive.

It is not, however, just technology, but also competition that has grown exponentially. Globalization, the rise of a shareholder value orientation, and the general surplus and prosperity of the developed world have all sharpened the competitive edge. Competition today comes from increasingly unexpected directions with, sometimes, massive impact. This forces companies to respond by producing more, better, faster, and cheaper, and this imperative places a premium on innovation.

Changes in attitude are also affecting modern companies. Trust and respect are in short supply and individualistic cultures that celebrate leadership will have to adapt to the mass death of deference. The very workers whose intellectual capital is the life-blood of the firm are precisely the ones who are least likely to respect hierarchy, incongruent values statements, and power distance. The dot.com phenomenon was an interesting example of people voting with their feet. Of course, it's not surprising that where the capital markets gave money away, bright young things followed.

HOW ORGANIZATIONS ARE RESPONDING

Learning to respond to breakneck change whilst courting ruthlessly discriminating customers and employees is the challenge of the opening years of the twenty-first century. Companies at the leading edge are beginning to organize their structures, people, and processes in new and different ways in order to accomplish this.

At a structural level there has been intense interest in business incubators and corporate venturing units. Incubators at CGNU (a UK financial services company) and Intel (a US microchip manufacturer) have been used to create an idea-flow of strategically relevant ideas that have some kind of synergy with the core business. For example, CGNU incubated a business called Assertahome.com that provides lifestyle home-related services that complement the mortgage and home loan services offered by the parent company. Typically these units exist outside of the heritage business unit structure in order to maximize their freedom of thought and speed of proposition development.

The corresponding problem of "legacy drag" – the slowness of moving new ideas through corporate structures – is a recurrent theme for many companies. The accretion of influence and resources by business units is largely dependent on the past and present market power of their existing goods, services, and business models. This tends to create a bias towards incremental product extensions and lead away from more radical creativity. This heritage bias demands a subtly different type of intellectual capital – the mindset for creativity and breakthrough is often very different to that required to deliver reliability and dependability. Additionally, business units frequently suffer from "Copernicus Syndrome" in which would-be innovators cannot get the hierarchy to back their innovation. Virgin claims to receive three ideas per day from innovators who could not get a hearing in their own companies.

Consequently, some companies are beginning to reform the way business units are organized. Virgin regards itself as a "branded venture capital group" and makes an effort to keep a "small company feel" inside each of its highly diversified businesses. Several computer manufacturing companies, including IBM, have broken up their business units into smaller and more nimble organizations. A European mobile phone company is currently considering aligning its organization around the core product development stages of: create, develop, and deliver; rather than market-facing units. Thus, one business unit leads product creation and development, another leads commercialization of new technologies and propositions, and a third focuses on providing service and operational excellence for mature propositions.

This innovation imperative is also driving a number of people-management changes. Enron (a US utility company) provides MBA-qualified new joiners with $50,000 to invest in new internal ventures. This practice diffuses capital allocation authority to relatively junior managers. Skandia focuses its values and culture management almost entirely towards innovation and Anheuser-Busch (a US brewer) has a team of young executives that "shadow" the executive committee. A number of other companies have developed phantom equity schemes that motivate innovation by allowing employees to share directly and proportionately in the value they create.

WHAT NEXT?

Although new products will continue to amaze and delight us, the greatest surprises may continue to be in the way that organizations change and develop. From a process perspective the main issues will remain speed and efficiency. There is, however, a limit as to how quickly you can develop and deliver a new product or service. Technology can certainly help to accelerate component pieces of the process, but the key barrier, decision-making, will continue to be more impacted by such issues as accountability, hierarchy, and capability – all linked to the organization.

Likewise, from a strategy perspective, even with a potential new wave of technological revolution, the key influence on success will not be in how financial support is determined, in how markets are segmented, or even in how portfolios are managed. The core issues will be twofold – how quickly a company can adapt to new environments and new challenges, and how well it manages and exploits its intellectual capital – again directly linked to the organization.

Going forward, it is the challenges of managing temporary expert networks, where knowledge is a transient commodity, that will drive innovation capability. How firms encourage, capture, exploit, and re-use the ideas and approaches that their employees, partners, or customers create or possess will be key. How organizations can build and share their intellectual property, acting both as a coherent cross-industry body to establish new technology platforms and standards, and simultaneously competing with their partners, will be a fundamental differentiator. Taking ideas to market will require more and more co-operation. It will demand ever-greater openness and trust. It will be driven by enthusiasm and motivation of individuals and, underpinning all of these, it will be facilitated by the flexibility of the organization.

KEY LEARNING POINTS

» In the last 20 years, attention has shifted not just onto product design, but onto the design of the organization itself as innovation capability has become a core competitive requirement. This change has been driven by an ever-increasing rate of technological change, increased competition, and changes in social attitude.

» Requirements for speed to market and unconstrained thinking have led many companies to establish incubator units whose job is to develop radical new products.

» Other companies are seeking to reform their business unit structures in order to reduce the "legacy drag" on new idea development.

» Companies are also beginning to use temporary expert networks to generate knowledge and new ideas from resources that are outside of the firm.

In Practice

Who should be looked at in demonstrating best practice right now? This chapter answers this by using three different examples of how companies are succeeding today:

» 3M's continued ability to conceive, develop, and launch a series of major innovations;
» Skandia's approach to creating an environment where innovation is the norm; and
» Zara's fast-track approach to idea delivery that is outstripping the competition.

There are numerous examples of best practice or successful approaches to taking ideas to market. Many of these have been mentioned elsewhere in the book but, for a more in-depth perspective, we have chosen three key organizations which we believe are leaders in their fields and demonstrate thinking and styles of managing the ideas to market conundrum provide valuable insights:

» 3M, widely promoted as a corporate leader in innovation, has been used to provide an understanding of some of the organizational issues in and around idea creation;
» Skandia, the Swedish insurance group, provides leadership in aligning the people within the organization and creating an environment in which innovation can occur; and
» Zara, the retail fashion group, has an impressive ability to benefit from an accelerated approach to taking its new designs to market faster than its competition.

3M – IDEA CREATION

"3M's distinguishing strength is its entrepreneurial drive to transform three dozen technology platforms into a constant and consistent new product flow, providing new solutions for new customers in new markets."

"3M's growth has come through a desire to participate in many markets where the company can make a significant contribution from core technologies, rather than be dominant in just a few markets."

3M annual report, 2000

"Hire good people and leave them alone." Now part of 3M's management philosophy, this statement is the foundation of the trust, innovation, and growth on which the company has been built and by which it continues to measure itself as it launches 500 new products each year.

3M, the US-based multinational, has for the past 100 years been seen as a leading organization that is consistently creating new ideas. As it has invented and reinvented numerous ideas, focused on its core capabilities and expanded across multiple sectors and created new technology platforms, and developed innovative products for both new and existing markets, 3M has gained a reputation as a global leader in taking ideas to market. There have been some bad patches, just like with any organization, but by and large, the reputation that has been built and promoted around 3M is well deserved. Through various different approaches adopted, the organization has developed an environment that encourages innovation. As it has evolved, it has gone the extra step in providing the necessary support culture, processes, and opportunities to really drive innovation and the creation of new ideas into the heart of the company.

3M – a brief history

3M, the Minnesota Mining & Manufacturing Company, was founded in 1902 in Two Harbors, Minnesota, on the shore of Lake Superior when five businessmen agreed to mine a mineral deposit for grinding-wheel abrasives. However, the deposits proved to be of little value, and the company quickly moved to nearby Duluth to focus on sandpaper products. Although there were several years of struggle, when the company gradually mastered quality production and built up a supporting supply chain, new investors were attracted to 3M and early technical and marketing innovations began to produce successes. The world's first waterproof sandpaper, designed to ease the health problem of sanding dust, was developed in the early 1920s and a major milestone occurred in 1925 with the invention of masking tape – an innovative step toward diversification and the first of many Scotch brand pressure-sensitive tapes.

In the next decade, technical progress resulted in Scotch™ Cellophane Tape for box-sealing, for which customers began to find many additional uses, including multiple consumer applications. Drawing on expertise in bonding mineral grit to sandpaper, 3M also brought out new adhesives to replace tacks in bonding upholstery, and sound-deadening materials for the auto industry's new metal-framed cars.

A roofing granule business was also developed in response to a need to make asphalt shingles last longer. In the early 1940s, 3M was diverted into defense materials for the Second World War, which was followed by new ventures, such as Scotchlite™ Reflective Sheeting for highway markings, magnetic sound recording tape, filament adhesive tape, and the start of 3M's involvement in the graphic arts with offset printing plates.

In the 1950s, 3M introduced the Thermo-Fax™ copying process, Scotchgard™ Fabric Protector, videotape, Scotch-Brite™ Cleaning Pads, and several new electromechanical products. In the 1960s dry-silver microfilm was introduced, photographic products, carbonless papers, overhead projection systems, and a rapidly growing health care business of medical and dental products. Markets further expanded in the 1970s and 1980s into pharmaceuticals, radiology, energy control, the office market, and globally to almost every country in the world. During the 1990s the company set new sales records of over $15bn annually.

In 2000 3M achieved record sales of $16.7bn and experienced one of the highest levels of innovation in its history, generating $5.6bn – nearly 35% of sales – from products introduced in the previous four years, with over $1.5bn of sales coming from products introduced in 2000 alone. To continue to drive this further, in the same year, 500 patents covering new innovations that will form the basis of future products for the company were filed by 3M in the US alone

Building a tradition of innovation

Creating an organization where such levels of innovation performance have become both expected and achieved has required clear focus on facilitating effective and continuous idea creation. Key to this has been the building of a supportive and motivating environment, something that 3M see as its "tradition of innovation." The six core elements of 3M's corporate culture that contribute to this tradition of innovation are:

» vision;
» foresight;
» stretch goals;
» empowerment;
» communication; and
» recognition.

Since the early days of the company, these six elements have been the drivers of continuous innovation and growth for the organization, and today, as the organization seeks to push itself to even higher levels of performance for its second century, they are still the fundamental backbone to the way in which 3M has defined and evolved the corporate culture to support successful idea creation.

Vision

The first element in creating the 3M tradition of innovation has been to declare the importance of innovation and make it part of the company's self-image. Hence the 3M vision to be "the world's most innovative enterprise and preferred supplier." Employees across the company are continuously reminded of this, and that their focus should be on achieving it. In addition, to consistently check that what the organization thinks it is doing is aligned to this vision, its customers are regularly consulted on their opinions about 3M and whether its claim to be the world's most innovative enterprise is true.

Foresight

Understanding customer needs, the trends in their industries, and the changes that are heading their way is also seen as a core element in 3M. However, this is far from easy, for reliably getting customers to indicate what there needs are, what are the problems that they encounter, and what solutions they might be looking for can be very difficult. The issue is that there are two levels of needs: the articulated kind – one where a customer recognizes it and can voice it openly; and the unarticulated need – problems that people do not know that they have. This second type is clearly far more difficult to find and, for 3M, this requires far greater insight into the customer's environment. However, although this is often much more difficult to capture, the rewards that stand to be gained from finding the unarticulated need, and then addressing it, can be very substantial. There are two examples that 3M like to talk about here to illustrate their success in this.

The first is salesman Dick Drew's recognition back in 1923 of the problems that automotive painters had in removing the tape that they used to hold masks in position during spraying. Although initially the articulated problem was seen to be one of how to repair any damaged paintwork after removal of the tape, he saw that the real problem was actually the tape itself. This led to the idea of a tape that was easier to remove and hence the invention of masking tape.

The second, 50 years later, is researcher Art Fry's matching-up of a problem of temporarily marking pages in a book with pieces of paper that unfortunately kept falling out, and a unique adhesive accidentally discovered by a colleague, Spence Silver. The adhesive was weak and did not stick very well, thus making it ineffective and unsuitable for the majority of applications. However, the resulting idea – having pieces of paper that could be stuck onto a surface and then removed with no residue or damage – did, after much experimentation and development, eventually lead to the final product: Post-it notes.

Stretch goals

The third core element in the building of 3M's innovation culture has been the adoption of a number of stretch goals designed to continuously push the organization further. There are two key goals that have been in place in the company for years, one focused on the medium term and the other more immediate.

» 3M had in place throughout the second half of the twentieth century the aim of deriving 30% of all sales from products introduced in the previous four years. This set the medium-term focus for the organization as it sought to achieve this target and when, in the late 1990s, achieving it became a regular occurrence, it was changed from 30% to an increased stretch goal of 35%, a target that a performance in 2000 of 33.5% came very near to achieving.

» To help achieve the improvement in this medium-term goal, there is also a more immediate target designed to create a sense of urgency across the company. For many years this was to have 10% sales from products introduced in only the last year and again, as performance increased, so this goal was increased in the late 1990s to 15%, a target which, by comparison, 2000 performance of 8.9% is some way off meeting. This goal is designed to ensure that the organization is more selective about what new ideas it pursues as it seeks to focus its resources on those that will provide the greatest return.

Empowerment

A fundamental element of the 3M philosophy is to give people responsibility and trust. William McKnight, who joined 3M in 1907, became president in 1929 and then chairman of the board in 1949, and is credited with first creating an environment within which innovation could occur, laid out two basic principles for empowerment of employees way back in 1948:

> "As our business grows, it becomes increasingly necessary to delegate responsibility and to encourage men and women to exercise their initiative. This requires considerable tolerance. Those men and women to whom we delegate authority and responsibility, if they are good people, are going to want to do their jobs in their own way."

As a guideline for this, all technical staff in 3M have, for the past 50 years, been encouraged to spend 15% of their time on projects of their own invention, giving them the time and space to experiment, make mistakes, learn, but most importantly feel in control of what they are doing and how important the organization believes this to be. The message is clear – if you have a good idea and the commitment to work on it, then go for it, even if it is at odds with 3M management. In essence the company has in some ways encouraged a healthy disrespect for management, specifically designed to allow people to pursue their own thing, rock the boat, but also potentially come up with something totally new for the company.

> "Mistakes will be made. But if a person is essentially right, the mistakes he or she makes are not as serious in the long run as the mistakes management will make if it undertakes to tell those in authority exactly how they must do their jobs. Management that is destructively critical when mistakes are made kills initiative, and it's essential that we have many people with initiative if we are to continue to grow."

Real empowerment also means toleration of mistakes, as people have to know that if they try something and it fails, they will not be punished. The alternative serves only to reduce risk-taking, taking the easy option, and never really being in the position to come up with anything radically new. This is true not only in the R&D world of 3M, where failures can sometimes be hidden, but also in the more visible areas of the company such as marketing. For every 1000 ideas only 100 are ever developed enough to be considered as projects, and only a few of these actually make it to launch. Even then, over 50% of new products launched onto the market are failures. This ratio is expected and hence the environment is designed to accommodate it, and to allow people to learn from their mistakes in the hope that the next time round, the insights gained will help improve the chances of success.

Communication

The fifth of 3M's core elements for creating a culture to support successful idea creation is open and extensive communication. This is three-way: management needs to communicate broad direction and vision to the labs; the labs need to be able to communicate new opportunities to management; marketing and innovators across the organization have to be able to communicate with one another. Indeed, a recent study of communication patterns within 3M showed that, unlike many organizations where the strongest communication typically occurs between operations, management, and sales, as they seek to maximize revenue from existing product and service lines, in 3M the dominant communication flows are between R&D, marketing, and senior management, as they drive forward new ideas to underpin the future of the company.

Of particular significance to 3M is communication across sectors and especially across technology platforms. One of the areas of great concern for the company in the late 1980s was an apparent stagnation as the varied divisions across the company – from health care to industrial tapes, and from data storage to office products – began to operate in silos as independent business units, each pursuing their individual aims. Although still successful, it was recognized that the opportunities for cross-business exploitation of new technologies were not being fully realized. Therefore, major efforts were made to further improve cross-business communication of new technology platforms with immediate effect: micro-replication technology, creating precise three-dimensional patterns on a variety of surfaces, began when 3M researchers were looking for improvements that could be made to a plastic lens in overhead projectors. The adoption of this technology allowed the subsequent plastic lens to perform better than the much heavier conventional glass lens. Since then, micro-replication has spread, first into other optical applications, such as more reflective material for traffic signs, and later in non-optical areas such as fasteners, connectors, and data storage discs.

To encourage this communication, the company has defined three basic ground rules:

» products belong to divisions but technologies belong to the company – they should, and must, be shared;
» multiple methods must be used for sharing information from intranet to technology forums and audits; and
» networking is the responsibility of everyone: if someone calls you, you are expected to spend your time helping them out.

Recognition

The final element in 3M's innovation culture is its system of reward and recognition. Foremost, the company does not believe in financial rewards: no huge bonuses are given to the best researchers as high performance innovation is expected from them. What the organization does do is recognize innovation in a very public manner and has several award programs covering all areas of the business, from R&D to marketing, to manufacturing and administration. For R&D there are a series of awards, partly determined by peer nomination. The ultimate is election to the Carlton Society – essentially the 3M hall of fame. Promotions are also a mechanism used in 3M in a different way. The company has adopted a dual-ladder career system where technical people have a choice. To progress, they can move into management, as is common in many organizations, or they can be promoted into more advanced technical positions. However, whichever option they choose, the salary, benefits, and other privileges are the same: promotion does not require people to move out of the areas of the company where they flourish into management – it is a choice.

KEY INSIGHTS

3M has created a corporate environment where idea creation is the norm, where innovation is expected, and where people both desire and feel able to take their ideas forward. How transferable this is to other organizations with an existing culture in place, or how well the six elements of vision, foresight, stretch goals, empowerment, communication, and recognition specifically apply to smaller companies, are both common questions asked by commentators. However, even if this cannot be completely replicated with the same levels of success, the underlying principles can be adopted by many other organizations. 3M recognizes that corporations must adapt and evolve if they expect to survive. Competitors will always bring products or technologies into the market that will change the basis of competition. To succeed, 3M has to be the company that innovates and the company that is at the forefront of idea creation.

That said, current performance is, however, not good enough for 3M, and after major restructuring in the mid-1990s and the spin-off of its data storage and imaging businesses, to further progress the organization is also currently driving several key initiatives across the entire company. These include:

» Global Products/Local Execution – ensuring people are able to work outside their home environments for three or more years to improve global thinking and execution and deliver new technology faster and more pervasively;
» Process Improvement – moving from multiple quality-management systems to one – Six Sigma – across the whole company to lower costs, increase sales, satisfy customers, develop managers, increase cash flow, and make the whole organization faster; and
» 3M Acceleration – targeting generating even greater return on the $1bn annual R&D investment by shortening development cycles and sharpening focus on growth areas with the best returns.

These are, however, all additional to the core of the organization which have for the past century, been at the heart of the company's continued success.

Table 7.1 3M Time-line.

1902	3M founded in Minnesota
1904	First sandpaper
1925	Masking tape
1930	Scotch^{TM} transparent tape
1935	First automotive under-seal coating
1939	First traffic sign using reflective sheeting
1954	Magnetic videotape
1956	Scotchgard^{TM} fabric and upholstery protector
1960	First sterile, disposable surgical drapes
1962	Tartan Track – first synthetic running track
1967	Disposable face masks
1972	Data cartridges revolutionize computer data storage
1979	Thinsulate^{TM} thermal insulation
1980	Post-It^{TM} notes
1985	Refastenable diaper tapes
1990	Fast connections for fiber-optic cables
1995	First medical aerosol without CFC propellant
1996	Brightness enhancement film improves laptop screens by 60%
1998	Flexible circuits for mobile phones
2000	Sandblaster sponges sand three times faster than sandpaper

Time-line

See Table 7.1.

SKANDIA – INNOVATION CULTURE

Skandia is one of the most innovative companies in financial services today. Established in 1855, Skandia was Sweden's first stock insurance company. Today the group holds euro 120bn in assets under management, employs 5600 staff, and is active in 20 countries worldwide.

Over the last decade, Skandia has consistently out-innovated most of its competitors in developing new and better investment and insurance products. The key to this has been a focused strategy and a deep commitment to people. Most companies would claim to have these things, but Skandia's difference amounts to much more than a corporate slogan.

In the early 1980s much of the asset management industry was highly vertically integrated. Companies performed fund management, product development, packaging, administration, and distribution in-house, and this model worked – proprietary funds represented 80% of sales in the US in 1980, but by the year 2000 they accounted for just 30% of sales.

Skandia's strategic revolution was to turn its attention purely to product development, packaging, and administration. It was the first financial services company to reject the industry wisdom of vertical integration. At the back end, it bought investment performance from a host of other fund managers and at the front end it left distribution to banks and financial advisors. The Skandia vision states "faster, smarter, better at helping our distributors serve their clients." This strategy has been refreshed and renewed by a consistent ability to set unreasonable goals as a way of driving corporate renewal. But focused strategy and unreasonable targets are only a part of what allows the group to make consistently high quality and innovative products.

The other part of Skandia's success is down to its people policies. Jan Carendi, Skandia's chairman, is the man who engineered the strategy, but most of what Jan talks about is people and, in particular, values, education, and renewal. "If you treat your people with warmth, charm, intimacy, and caring they will ruthlessly destroy your competitors." A key belief in Skandia is that a truly innovative and entrepreneurial culture is a vital competitive asset. This is accomplished in a number of ways. Skandia's balanced scorecard includes a focus on human factors that is almost exclusively concerned with the extent to which employees feel that managers and peers contribute to the innovative culture. This survey is backed up with a strong commitment to the accountability of line managers for the culture of their work units. Over-performance can be used as a way to identify and share knowledge, whilst identified under-performance is used as a catalyst for development and feedback.

Despite the precision of Skandia's values-based scorecarding, a key assumption for the company is that building control systems is just as expensive as investing in building employees' understanding. As Carendi says, "if you think competence costs a lot – try incompetence." Learning at Skandia is both a strategic priority and a managed process, and it is combined with the recognition that quality learning does not come cheaply. Skandia's scorecard, for example, captures the *per capita* cost of training and development.

Education is a part of what enables the process of continual renewal. Carendi talks about the challenge of "turning around a successful company." Many companies lose out when success breeds complacency and boom turns to bust. To achieve repeated and extraordinary success requires a suffusion of collective wisdom into the culture, structure, and systems of the organization – "no one is more clever than everyone," as Carendi puts it. In practice, this means a continual critical re-examination of past assumptions to avoid becoming blinded by success.

Whilst Skandia stands as an example of strategic focus as a way of building success, its real point of differentiation is its powerful focus on values-based management and education to create a culture that is a genuine source of competitive advantage.

KEY INSIGHTS

Skandia's success rests on innovation, strategic discipline, and culture. As a strategy, the group's focus on product packaging and administration allows it to concentrate on areas of greatest opportunity. However, it takes genuine bravery and belief to run in the opposite direction to the rest of the industry, which in the mid-1980s was highly vertically integrated. This ability has been reinforced by a willingness to set unreasonable goals.

Much of Skandia's management effort is focused on the development of a culture élan that supports the company's ability to build and maintain profitable relationships with intermediaries and to be consistently innovative. Values and culture is much more than a slogan at Skandia. Senior managers are genuinely committed and HR systems are highly focused. A similar rigor is brought to the learning process.

In summary, Skandia's success stems from:

» a differentiated and focused strategy;
» a willingness both to take risks and to set unreasonable goals; and

> » a congruent set of systems that builds and supports an innovative and customer-focused culture.

Time-line

See Table 7.2.

Table 7.2 Skandia Time-line.

1855	Skandia founded in Sweden, as the country's first stock insurance company
1863	Lists on the Stockholm Stock Exchange
1900	Skandia enters US market
1986	Creation of Skandia AFS, specialist in co-operation concept
1993	Implements the internal balanced scorecard including intellectual capital measures
1997	Leif Edvinsson, receives award for innovation

HOT COUTURE AT THE HOUSE OF ZARA

What was started in 1963 as a small lingerie manufacturing company in Northern Spain with a mere $25 starting capital is today one of the world's fastest-growing fashion businesses. Not only is Zara rapidly increasing its share of the market, but it is also changing the way high-street fashion retailers go about doing their business. Zara has shelved traditional fashion logic and approach – there are no four seasons at Zara to adhere to, only continuous changes with stores receiving new stock every two weeks.

From lingerie to high-street fashion

The high-street fashion chain Zara was founded by Amancio Ortega, initially to sell lingerie and pajamas, but soon the entrepreneur expanded into high-street fashion and the first Zara store was opened in 1975. Today, Zara has some 450 stores worldwide and is looking at expanding with around 150 stores a year. Inditext, of which Zara is subsidiary, floated on the Madrid Stock Exchange in May 2001, making

Ortega Spain's richest man. The company's stock was oversubscribed 27 times and raised some $1.8bn for the initial share sale of a 23% stake in the company. This was at a time when retail fashion shares were doing less well in a market where the economic slow-down was hitting spending, and European retailers were laying off employees to deter the flailing profits.

The company has to maintain its competitive edge to continue to succeed in a market where customers are fickle and margins are easily squashed by mistakes in the design-to-stock process. Although Inditex is more profitable than its competitors, earning $0.99 on every euro 10 in sales, compared to Hennes & Mauritz's euro 84 and GAP's euro 64, it has to attract more shoppers to keep the sales growing in its expanded network of stores.

The Zara brand is aimed at fashion-conscious young individuals who see clothing as perishables – what is fashionable today will inevitably be out-of-date tomorrow; designs are worn just as long as they are credible amongst peers. This emphasizes the need for Zara to keep in touch with the customer. If it fails at this and at delivering what the customers want fast, the people who keep Zara's revenue growing will move to the next store along the high street.

The approach to design – faster, more, and by imitating

Zara's headquarters in La Coruña is the home for the company's design team, the 200 designers who are responsible for selecting the right colors, materials, and shapes for the clothes to be supplied to the stores. What differentiates Zara from its main rivals and peers – the Swedish Hennes & Mauritz (H&M), GAP, and the like – is the incredible speed at which designs are taken from concept to final product in-store. This can, at H&M, take as long as nine to ten months, whereas Zara manages the same within a month, sometimes in as little as two weeks.

Zara also maintains an image of always having its finger on the pulse of the latest fads and fashion must-haves, by providing its customers with an ever-changing selection of clothes. Zara's production is in-house and this enables the company to effectively test how designs are doing in the stores. If a certain design is not selling, then it can easily be changed to accommodate customer demand. Often stores are only supplied with a small number of a certain design – if it sells well, the production of this item is accelerated and the stores supplied with more merchandise. This effectively means that Zara tests its products in stores rather than at a pre-launch stage.

As the company can change designs based on the reaction they gained in the stores, mistakes have less of an impact on the final bottom line. As the designs and what is supplied in the stores are so much dependent on customer say, the number of the designs that are not welcomed by customers and consequently have to be sold at discount are fewer than industry average. Any items that fail to attract the customers can be changed within Zara, and later supplied to the stores, with an enhanced design.

Zara's designers follow the market-place both by meticulously studying the fashion shows and the high street; Zara knows that its customers are influenced by the expensive *prêt-à-porter* lines of the fashion houses in Milan, Paris, and London, but they also interpret designs to accommodate their lifestyles and thus become a fashion force of their own. These are Zara's influences – the top-down supply of fashion and the customer view of these. Zara simply provides its customers with new designs more often than its rivals – and at that speed, it still manages to provide what customers want.

Process – in-house and integrating the customer

Zara has succeeded in taking the customer to the center of its design process and thereafter vertically integrating the entire production process to ensure that the right designs are reaching the right stores at the right time. Mistakes are, of course, made, but these are rectified quickly – based on feedback from the network of stores, Zara's production can change the color or add new details to a design and thus ensure that it is what will sell.

All Zara's stores are linked to the headquarters with a computerized communication system that allows personnel to share ideas and input customer feedback and reactions. This information is then shared with the headquarters and this allows the adjustment of volume and style of orders to accommodate shifts in customer demand. Zara aims at keeping the company's image an up-to-date and fresh one through being close to the customers – this also limits the mistakes made in the designs, and through having more than one delivery per month the company sees what is selling and can pull any designs that do not sell quickly enough. Zara minimizes inventory, and thus keeps operating costs down.

Zara integrates all stages of value-creation in the design and processing of fabrics, manufacturing of garments, and in the sale process. Approximately half of the clothes are manufactured in plants owned by Inditex. Some 80% of garments are manufactured in Europe – mainly in Spain and Portugal.

Logistics – speed-to-market

To survive in a competitive market, it is no longer enough to buy the right goods at the right cost – retailers must also get them to the right place at the right time, and within the right operational costs. Doing this well requires the best possible logistics, combining the information that determines buying decisions with the product flows that get goods to customers more efficiently (*The McKinsey Quarterly*, 1996, No.2–"Retail logistics: one size doesn't fit all").

From the beginning, Zara has kept the logistics as a core capability essential to being able to supply the merchandise at the right time. This is one of the reasons that Zara maintains its production centers mainly in Europe; this cuts the delivery time and cost to minimum, albeit possibly not allowing for the cheapest production of the merchandise. With the logistics that deliver fast, the overall strategy of "fashion now" is strengthened.

Zara's main distribution center is located in La Coruña, north-west Spain, from where merchandise is shipped to all the stores several times a week. In Europe, fleets of trucks deliver the merchandise, covering a distance of more than 7 million kilometers a year. Shipments to more distant stores are made by air-freight, thereby cutting the time between the placement of the order and the reception of the merchandise (Inditex Annual Report, 2000).

Tapping into the consumer's mind

Zara provides fashion considerably quicker than any of its rivals: this is what the company's success is based on. A sketch of a design can be in the stores as quickly as within a few weeks. Aiming at producing fashion designs that are regarded in the same manner as previously foodstuffs were, i.e. items that are perishable, Zara succeeds in creating a company that exists to supply for the fashion-conscious who may or may not use a design more than once.

Zara has managed to expand and gain market-share in a highly competitive industry at uncertain times through disregarding traditional fashion logic. The company updates its designs at a continuous pace, rather than focusing on seasons, as traditional fashion retailers have done. Zara is putting its customers at the center of the design and production process, through the computer network that connects all stores and by which customers' feedback and response to designs are fed to both the manufacturing and the business sides of Zara, and volumes and design can thus be altered.

The speed at which Zara brings designs to market, be they imitations of the catwalk or in-house creations inspired by current trends on the streets and clubs of Europe, is what at the moment allows Zara to expand at its ambitious pace. And as Inditex's CEO José Mará Castellano highlights: "this business is all about reducing response time" (*CNET Investor*, May 23, 2001).

KEY INSIGHTS

Zara, the Spanish fashion retailer, is rapidly increasing its share of the market, and it is at the same time changing the way high-street fashion retailers go about doing their business. Zara has chosen to ignore established methods of shelving traditional fashion with its seasons. Zara adheres to no fashion logic – it renews its stock twice a month.

What differentiates Zara from its main competitors – the Swedish H&M and the US clothing chain GAP – is its ability to deliver the latest fashion at a much faster speed – whereas it takes H&M nine to ten months to deliver new designs, it only takes Zara some four weeks, sometimes even as little as two. This is what provides the company with its competitive advantage and has allowed it to grow at such an impressive pace and at the same time build investor confidence in its future.

Zara's production is in-house, which enables the company to effectively test the designs in its stores before a large-scale launch. Often stores are only supplied with a small number of each design – if the merchandise sells well, the stores will be supplied with more merchandise; if not, the design will be pulled. This effectively means that Zara tests new designs in-store, rather than at a pre-launch stage.

Time-line

See Table 7.3.

Table 7.3 Zara Time-line.

1963	Amancio Ortega opens a shop in La Coruña, north-west Spain, selling lingerie and pajamas.
1975	The first Zara shop is opened in La Coruña
1984	José Mará Castellano from IBM joins Inditex
1985	The creation of Inditex as head of the Group
1988	The first Zara store outside Spain is opened in Portugal
1989	The first US store is opened in New York, and an outlet in Paris is opened
1991	Zara has been expanded to four countries
2000	Zara is present in 30 countries, 450 stores
2001	Inditex, the group to which Zara belongs, is floated, the stock market being 27 times oversubscribed

Key Concepts and Thinkers

Who are the key people and what have they contributed to the world of innovation? This chapter identifies the major contributors in three core areas:

» creativity;
» process; and
» strategy.

Taking ideas to market is clearly a wide and varied subject. It covers multiple aspects from creativity and innovation strategy through to product launch and enabling organizations. Within this arena there are many researchers, industry leaders, and service providers who have developed an increasingly diverse range of conceptual models focused on improving the chances of success and making the process both more effective and more efficient. From this body of knowledge, we have selected 11 key people whose thoughts and ideas have, we feel, made a significant contribution to the advancement of practice. Although clearly overlapping in certain areas, three of these, Edward de Bono, John Kao and Teresa Amabile, are focused on creativity, three, Bob Cooper, Scott Edgett and Abbie Griffin, concentrate more on the core processes, and the other five, Gary Hamel, Clayton Christensen, Michael McGrath, Joe Tidd, and Peter Drucker address strategic issues concerned with innovation and new ideas.

EDWARD DE BONO – CREATIVE THINKING

Regarded by many as the world's leading authority in the field of conceptual and creative thinking, Edward de Bono is the author of 62 books and is the originator of lateral thinking, which treats creativity as the behavior of information in a self-organizing information system – such as neural networks in the brain. Edward de Bono has experience from working with a number of organizations from a wide spectrum of industries for over 25 years. He runs international seminars on creative thinking. Embraced by the media as a guru in creativity, he is best known for his key works: *Six Hats*, *Lateral Thinking*, and *I am Right You are Wrong*.

Creativity is becoming increasingly important for all businesses in an environment where competition intensifies and the pace of change accelerates. As a consequence, it is crucial that organizations continue to add value and operate in a more efficient way. In *Serious Creativity* (1992), Edward de Bono provides an overview of many of his key concepts and thinking, and introduces the reader to systematic tools and techniques that can be used to enhance creativity. Furthermore, de Bono brings together some of the learnings from *Six Hats* and *Lateral Thinking*, as well as the practical application of these techniques.

Throughout the book, de Bono brings in examples on how a different, lateral, approach has impacted the bottom line for organizations, such as Heinz and Prudential.

Link

Edward de Bono
www.edwdebono.com

JOHN KAO – DRIVING CREATIVITY IN THE BUSINESS ENVIRONMENT

John Kao is founder and CEO of The Idea Factory in California and author of *Jamming: The Art and Discipline of Business Creativity*, a *Business Week* bestseller that has been translated into over 20 languages. For 14 years, he was a professor at Harvard Business School where he developed and taught courses on innovation and entrepreneurship for the MBA program. In addition, he was a visiting professor at the MIT Media Lab and chair of the 45th International Design Conference in Aspen. For the past three years he has also been academic director of the Managing Innovation executive program at Stanford University.

In *Jamming*, Kao emphasizes that companies that understand the importance of managing creativity and the effective organization of the output from creative processes will help survival in today's competitive environment. The book gives examples on how to build a stimulating environment in which employees are motivated to work towards a common goal, free of preconceptions. Kao demonstrates successes and failures in companies' use of creative resources through example case studies. His other publications include *Entrepreneurship*, *Creativity and the Organization*, *Managing Creativity*, *The Entrepreneur*, and *The Entrepreneurial Organization*.

In addition to his work in creativity, John Kao is also actively involved in the entertainment industry. He was production executive on Steven Soderbergh's breakthrough *Sex, Lies and Videotape*, and producer of the Broadway play *Golden Child*, which was nominated for three Tony awards.

Link

The Idea Factory
www.theideafactory.com

TERESA M. AMABILE – ORGANIZATIONAL CREATIVITY AND MOTIVATION

Teresa Amabile is the Edsel Bryant Ford Professor of Business Administration at Harvard Business School and is the leading academic researcher in the field of organizational creativity. Initially educated and employed as a chemist, she received her PhD in psychology from Stanford University in 1977. Originally focusing on individual creativity, Amabile's research has expanded to encompass team creativity and organizational innovation. This 25-year program of research on how the work environment can influence creativity and motivation has yielded a theory of creativity and innovation; methods for assessing creativity, motivation, and the work environment; and a set of prescriptions for maintaining and stimulating innovation.

Teresa Amabile is the author of *Creativity in Context* and *Growing up Creative*, as well as over 100 papers, chapters, and presentations. In *Creativity in Context*, she provides a detailed analysis of the social factors that enhance and impede creativity in schools, art, and business, and provides a theory of motivation and creativity that captures the complex ways in which both intrinsic and extrinsic motivation can interact to enhance creativity. This book offers insights into how organizations influence creativity and provides a tool for the assessment of organizational climates for creativity.

Teresa Amabile serves on the editorial boards of *Academy of Management Journal*, *Creativity Research Journal*, *Creativity and Innovation Management*, and *Journal of Creative Behavior*. Her recent papers include: *Motivational Synergy: Toward New Conceptualizations of Intrinsic and Extrinsic Motivation in the Workplace*, *Assessing the Work Environment for Creativity*, and *Changes in the Work Environment for Creativity During Downsizing*.

Link

Center for Creative Leadership
www.ccl.org

ROBERT G. COOPER – STAGEGATE PROCESSES, SUCCESS FACTORS, AND PROJECT SELECTION

Bob Cooper is Professor of Industrial Marketing and Technology Management at the Michael G. DeGroote School of Business, McMaster University in Ontario, Canada, and is widely seen as a world expert in the field of new product management. He is the author of 75 papers and articles and five books. Honored numerous times, the Product Development Management Association made Bob the Third Crawford Fellow in 1998.

He is best known as the creator of the stage-gate process that is now widely used by organizations across the world to help them take their ideas from concept to market. This approach divides the development process into a number of key phases, each of which are separated by key decision points or gates. It has been adopted and adapted by many organizations and has proven to lead to improved quality, greater speed, and more focus on maximizing value creation. *Winning at New Products: Accelerating the Process from Idea to Launch*, his most popular book, is now in its tenth printing and has sold over 40,000 copies. It provides a detailed overview on how to implement a stage-gate process.

Cooper is also recognized as one of the pioneers in the field of what differentiates between success and failure in developing and launching new products and services. His NewProd computer program, based on his extensive research into the core success factors, has also been adopted by many companies to help them with some of the key up-front decisions driving product selection. *Product Leadership: Creating and Launching Superior New Products*, his most recent book, brings together many of his concepts and illustrates them with numerous examples from clients and research partners, including Polaroid, Dow Chemical, Du Pont, Hewlett Packard, IBM, Guinness, and American Express. Going beyond the process level, this brings issues of strategy and leadership into scope.

Together with his colleague Scott Edgett, Bob Cooper is also director of the Product Development Institute, a consulting organization based in Canada.

Links

Management of Innovation and New Technology, McMaster University
www.mint.mcmaster.ca
Product Development Institute
www.prod-dev.com

SCOTT EDGETT – PROJECT SELECTION AND PORTFOLIO MANAGEMENT

A colleague of Bob Cooper, Scott Edgett is also an Associate Professor or Marketing at the Michael G. DeGroote School of Business, McMaster University in Ontario, Canada. Having co-authored several books with Bob Cooper, Scott is known for his work in project selection and portfolio management. Scott is CEO of the Product Development Institute.

Portfolio Management for New Products is his most recognized book and provides a detailed overview of tools for linking product development to strategy and ensuring that, from idea to launch, resources are deployed efficiently. This offers an analytical approach to managing a portfolio of projects, as you would a financial portfolio.

In conjunction with software supplier Sopheon, the Product Development Institute has created Accolade, a generic automated stage-gate version of the stage-gate process, to help decision-making and cross-functional communication. This can be tailored to individual organizations' process requirements, and includes NewProd 3000, a diagnostic tool for evaluating and prioritizing new ideas at the early stages of development.

Links

Product Development Institute
www.prod-dev.com
Sopheon
www.sopheon.com

ABBIE GRIFFIN – MEASURING PRODUCT DEVELOPMENT PERFORMANCE

Abbie Griffin is Professor of Business Administration at the University of Illinois and Editor of the *Journal of Product Innovation Management*, the leading publication in the field. Her research focuses on measuring and improving the new product development process and she has authored many related papers. Prior to becoming an academic she worked at both Corning and Polaroid and was a consultant with Booz, Allen and Hamilton.

Griffin's key papers have covered such issues as modeling and measuring product development cycle-time, recommended measures for product development success and failure, measuring product development to improve quality, and best practice for customer satisfaction. She also conducted a major benchmarking exercise on new product development performance for the Product Development and Management Association (PDMA).

Griffin was a senior editor of the *PDMA Handbook of New Product Development*, the leading reference guide for all aspects of the development process. Providing a collection of practical tools, processes, advice, and skills-sets that can enhance product development performance, this is an all-in-one picture of product development today and has become the key book for many executives responsible for taking new products and services from concept to launch.

Links

University of Illinois
www.uinc.edu
Product Development and Management Association
www.pdma.org

GARY HAMEL – REINVENTING YOUR ORGANIZATION AND RECREATING BUSINESS CONCEPTS

Gary Hamel is Visiting Professor of Strategic and International Management at the London Business School and Chairman of Strategos, an international consulting company. He is a world-renowned business thinker, arguably one of the leading strategy gurus of today, and author of two of the key texts impacting how organizations develop and exploit their ideas: *Competing for the Future* and *Leading the Revolution*.

Competing for the Future was *Business Week's* management book of the year and has appeared on every management bestseller list. Co-authored with C.K. Prahalad, it is based on their award-winning *HBR* article *The Core Competence of the Organization*, and focuses on how organizations can transform their industry by creating their own futures and reinventing themselves.

In *Leading the Revolution*, his most recent book, Hamel argues that companies miss opportunities for creating new wealth by emphasizing the stewardship and optimization of existing business models. The solution that he proposes is to create internal "free markets" for ideas, capital, and people. These markets work by attraction, not allocation, so that resources naturally configure around opportunities. By contrast, resources in most large companies are tightly planned and controlled, and Hamel argues that this is ultimately a question of business philosophy, of stewardship, or entrepreneurship. Stewardship activities are aimed at eliminating downside risk and generating efficiencies. Entrepreneurship activities are aimed at maximizing upside risk and creating new products, markets, and even industries.

He contrasts a typical venture capital firm receiving 5000 business plans a year with a typical company director receiving five or fewer. Part of the problem is that the corporate innovator not only has to battle through a skeptical hierarchy but also faces little real reward when his approved plan is successful. By contrast, a successful entrepreneur will be a millionaire many times over. Furthermore, he can go to many different venture capital firms to fund his idea, whereas a single "no" anywhere up the chain of command can kill a corporate innovation.

Links

Strategos
www.strategos.com
Leading the Revolution homepage
www.leadingtherevolution.com

CLAYTON M. CHRISTENSEN – BENEFITING FROM DISRUPTIVE TECHNOLOGIES

Clayton Christensen is a professor of business administration at the Harvard Business School and author of *The Innovator's Dilemma*, which received the *Global Business* Book Award for the best business book published in 1997. His research and teaching interests center on the management of technological innovation, developing organizational capabilities, and finding new markets for new technologies. Christensen's writings have been published in the *Wall Street Journal*, the *Harvard Business Review*, *Business History Review*, *Research Policy*, *Industrial and Corporate Change*, *Strategic Management Journal*, *Production and Operations Management*, the *European Management Journal*, *Management Science*, and *Engineering Management Review*. He advises corporations concerning their management of technological innovation.

In *The Innovator's Dilemma*, Christensen shows what the Honda Supercub, Intel's 8088 processor, and hydraulic excavators have in common. They are all examples of disruptive technologies that helped to redefine the competitive landscape of their respective markets. These products did not come about as the result of successful companies carrying out sound business practices in established markets. Christensen shows how these and other products cut into the low end of the market-place and eventually evolved to displace high-end competitors and their reigning technologies.

At the heart of *The Innovator's Dilemma* is how a successful company with established products keeps from being pushed aside by newer, cheaper products that will, over time, get better and become a serious threat. Christensen proposes that even the best-managed companies, in spite of their attention to customers and continual investment in new technology, are susceptible to failure no matter what the industry, be it hard drives or consumer retailing.

Link
Harvard Business School – Executive Education
www.exed.hbs.edu

MICHAEL MCGRATH – PRODUCT STRATEGY FOR HIGH-TECH COMPANIES

Michael McGrath was one of the founding directors of Pittiglio Rabin Todd & McGrath (PRTM), a consulting company focused on new product development and supply chain management, and is author of three books, *Product Development: Success through Product and Cycle-time Excellence*, *Product Setting the PACE in Product Development* and *Product Strategy for High-Technology Companies*.

The first two of these are guides to product and cycle-time excellence, PRTM's approach to product development. This brings together the firm's version of a phase review development process with issues such as decision-making, team organization, activity structure, development tools, product strategy, technology management, and pipeline management.

Product Strategy for High-Technology Companies is more a strategic guide focused on the key elements required for an effective and coherent product strategy. It addresses how to develop a product strategy within a technology-driven business, understanding the impact of generic strategies from others' experience, the skills necessary to formulate a competitive strategy, and how to manage the product strategy process.

Link

PRTM
www.prtm.com

JOE TIDD – MANAGING MULTIPLE DIMENSIONS OF INNOVATION

Joe Tidd is Professor of Technology and Innovation Management at the Science and Technology Policy Research Unit (SPRU) at the University of Sussex, England. He was previously director of the Executive MBA Programme and head of the Management of Innovation Group at Imperial College, London.

The author of four books, Tidd is one of the leading UK academics in the innovation field. A policy advisor to the Confederation of British Industry (CBI), where he launched the CBI Innovation Trends Survey, he also works as a consultant with Arthur D. Little, Cap Gemini Ernst & Young, and McKinsey. He is managing editor of the *International Journal of Innovation Management*.

In *Managing Innovation: Integrating Technological, Market and Organizational Change* (Wiley), Tidd and his co-authors, John Bessant and Keith Pavitt, take an integrative and holistic approach to the management of innovation, addressing the fields of technology, market, and organizational innovation. The focus is on three core themes: the identification and development of core competencies; the constraints imposed by different technologies and markets; and the structures and processes for organizational learning.

Links

SPRU
www.susx.ac.uk/spru
CBI Innovation Trends Survey
www.cbi.org.uk/innovation

PETER F. DRUCKER – INNOVATION AND ENTREPRENEURSHIP

Peter Drucker is a writer, teacher, and consultant specializing in strategy and policy for businesses and social sector organizations. He has consulted with many of the world's largest corporations as well as with non-profit organizations, small and entrepreneurial companies, and with agencies of the US government. He has also worked with the governments of Canada, Japan, and Mexico. He is the author of 31 books that have been translated into more than 20 languages. Thirteen books deal with society, economics, and politics; 15 deal with management. Two of his books are novels, one is autobiographical, and he is a co-author of a book on Japanese painting. He has made four series of educational films based on his management books. He has been an editorial columnist for the *Wall Street Journal* and a frequent contributor to the *Harvard Business Review* and other periodicals.

Peter Drucker has been hailed in the United States and abroad as the seminal thinker, writer, and lecturer on the contemporary organization. In 1997, he was featured on the cover of *Forbes* magazine under the headline, "Still the Youngest Mind," and *Business Week* has called him "the most enduring management thinker of our time."

Drucker's *Innovation and Entrepreneurship* focuses on the "what, where, and when" of management; it studies different aspects affecting both innovation and entrepreneurship in an organization, such as risks, opportunities, strategies and staffing, compensation, and reward mechanisms. The book stresses that innovation and entrepreneurship are skills that can be learnt and systematically applied to benefit an organization.

Link

Peter F. Drucker Foundation
www.pfdf.org

Resources

So where can you go for help? Who are useful sources of knowledge and insight? This chapter identifies 16 organizations and publications in five areas:

» US-based organizations;
» UK-based organizations;
» academically-linked groups;
» consultancy-linked groups; and
» international publications.

There is a wealth of organizations and publications that provide data, information, insights, and expertise that can help you take your ideas to market. Some of these are national, some global in scope and reach, some are linked to academia, and others focus purely on the business world. We have selected 16 varied key resources that can provide useful input to your organization as you seek to drive innovation and the ability to deliver new concepts to your customers. Three of these, the PDMA, the ACA, and the DMI are US-based international non-profit professional bodies; three, the Design Council, the Chartered Institute of Marketing and the CBI, are UK-based organizations; five, the Center for Innovation in Product Development, the Center for Creative Leadership, the Cambridge Network, the London Business School Innovation Forum, and CranfieldCreates, are academically related groups; two, the Strategos Institute and the Cap Gemini Ernst & Young Center for Business Innovation, are consultancy-linked organizations; and three, the *Journal of Product Innovation Management*, *Technology Review*, and *Red Herring* are international publications.

PRODUCT DEVELOPMENT AND MANAGEMENT ASSOCIATION

Founded in 1976, the Product Development and Management Association (PDMA) is a volunteer-driven, non-profit organization. About 80% of its members are corporate practitioners of new product development, with the remaining 20% split evenly between academics and service providers. The organization is based in the US but has activities worldwide including a major presence in the UK. The PDMA's mission is to improve the effectiveness of people engaged in developing and managing new products – both new manufactured goods and new services. This mission includes facilitating the generation of new information, helping convert this information into knowledge that is in a usable format, and making this new knowledge broadly available to those who might benefit from it. A basic tenet of the Association is that enhanced product innovation represents a desirable and necessary economic goal for firms that wish to achieve and retain a profitable competitive advantage in the long term.

The PDMA actively supports several knowledge-generating activities. It sponsors a yearly research competition and rewards up to three proposals with financial support and research access to PDMA members. PDMA has sponsored a yearly PhD Proposal Competition since 1991 to encourage young academics to engage in new product development research. Finally, PDMA has directly supported three streams of research over the last eight years, resulting in several papers and many presentations of the findings: *Profiles and Compensation of New Product Professionals* (Feldman, 1991, 1996), *Measuring Product Development Success* (Griffin and Page, 1993, 1996), and *Trends and Best Practices in the Practice of Managing New Product Development* (Page, 1993; Griffin 1997).

Knowledge-disseminating activities include an annual international conference on the general subject of new product development. The Association publishes the highly-rated *Journal of Product Innovation Management* six times a year. In addition to this, *Visions*, a newsletter, is published quarterly and distributed to all PDMA members. The Association has published *The PDMA Handbook of New Product Development* (John Wiley & Sons, 1996), which comprehensively covers the latest developments and insights in new product development from a managerial point of view.

Links

www.pdma.org
www.pdma.org.uk

AMERICAN CREATIVITY ASSOCIATION

The American Creativity Association (ACA) is a non-profit organization dedicated to promoting increased awareness of the importance of creativity to society and to encouraging the development of personal and professional creativity.

The ACA constitutes members from a wide background representing many a different domain. The Association provides the forum in which to exchange ideas, experiences, and learnings. One of the founding principles of the organization was to create a network of individuals that represents different fields of interests and backgrounds. The ACA is consequently organized into four multi-disciplinary societies: Business & Industry, Communications & the Arts, Education & Training, and Science & Technology. These societies provide the members with the opportunity to interact with those who have common interests and thus cross-share and disseminate knowledge.

The ACA publishes *FOCUS*, a bi-monthly newsletter that includes the latest trends, events, and member activities in the field of creativity. The Association also sponsors national conventions and regional meetings to aid the cross-fertilization of knowledge.

Link

www.amcreativityassoc.org

DESIGN MANAGEMENT INSTITUTE

The non-profit organization, Design Management Institute (DMI) was founded in Boston, Massachusetts, in 1975. The organization is dedicated to the demonstrating and promoting the strategic importance of design in business and to improving the management and utilization of design. In addition, the organization seeks to improve the management and utilization of design. The Institute's programs aid design managers in becoming leaders in their professions, as well as in educating and fostering interaction among design professionals, organizational managers, public policy makers, and academics.

The DMI has several ongoing activities that support and facilitate improved design in all aspects of life, from new products and services to government activities and education, including:

» three award programs honoring excellence in design management;
» a case study program focused on developing teaching case studies in the classic Harvard Business School format – 35 are available and are used in 200 business schools worldwide;
» the International Forum on Design Management Research and Education is an annual conference designed to facilitate improved communication and collaboration between education and design practice; and
» the *DMI Academic Review* is a major journal that disseminates the latest ideas and concepts across both business and academic arenas.

Link

www.dmi.org

DESIGN COUNCIL

The Design Council, a UK-based non-profit organization, identifies, develops, and promotes best use of design to improve competitiveness and to fuel economic growth and British success. Founded in 1944, the Design Council has, for over 50 years, been striving to promote the effective use of design – and design thinking – in business, in education, and in government. The Design Council is independent of the government and is run as an autonomous, non-profit public body funded by the Department of Trade and Industry.

The Design Council enhances the interaction between design professionals and the cross-sharing of expertise through the series of lectures on a wide-ranging field of topics running through the year. These are often aimed at provoking debate and thus adding to the thinking and development of knowledge. In addition to these seminars, the Design Council also runs and develops events, exhibitions, TV programs, publications, and research.

The Design Council aims at helping UK businesses to understand and to use design as a central part of their business strategies to drive competitiveness. The Design Council works with a number of partners from industry.

Link

www.design-council.org.co.uk

CHARTERED INSTITUTE OF MARKETING

The Chartered Institute of Marketing (CIM) provides leadership and expertise for those involved in marketing. As the world's largest marketing association, the CIM works closely with the marketing profession, government, industry, and commerce to develop greater understanding of what and how marketing contributes to UK and international business.

The CIM has expanded to include six international branches and four member groups, in addition to the 58 branches and market interest groups in the UK. All in all, the CIM has some 60,000 members. The Institute provides professional qualifications up to postgraduate level through some 350 colleges and universities worldwide. Furthermore, it provides marketing professionals with residential training courses – these are designed to be flexible and designed to meet different corporate needs. The CIM also operates a consultancy service and a comprehensive information service.

Link

www.cim.co.uk

CONFEDERATION OF BRITISH INDUSTRY

The Confederation of British Industry (CBI) is the UK's leading independent business organization and exists so that the government of the day, the European Commission, and the wider community understand both the needs of British business and the contribution it makes to the well-being of UK society.

CBI's Innovation Trends survey was initiated in 1989 to gauge companies' perceptions of, and attitude towards, innovation. The survey is undertaken in co-operation with industry sponsors and provides a wealth of information for both business representatives and academics.

Link

www.cbi.org.uk

CENTER FOR INNOVATION IN PRODUCT DEVELOPMENT

The Center for Innovation in Product Development is one of the key research centers in the US. Based at MIT, it seeks to unite representatives from academia, industry, and government who share its vision of the future of product development. Its mission is to lay the conceptual groundwork for, and contribute core components to, a product development infrastructure that helps companies to succeed in the services market-place we envision.

Link

http://me.mit.edu/groups/cipd

CENTER FOR CREATIVE LEADERSHIP

The Center for Creative Leadership (CCL) is a recognized, non-profit educational institution, acting as a resource for enhancing the understanding of the leadership capabilities of individuals and organizations alike. The Center believes that leadership development is a cornerstone of organizational effectiveness and addresses the leadership components of both organizational and business challenges.

The CCL has been in operation for more than 30 years and has during this time created programs and services blending relevant models, research, assessment tools, and expertise with proven tools and techniques aimed at enhancing learning.

The CCL provides executive education in a number of fields, ranging from fostering innovation and merging cultures to working globally. In addition, it also has a wealth of information and materials, which, together with the other services, provide a source of knowledge within the field of leadership.

Link

www.ccl.org

THE CAMBRIDGE NETWORK

The Cambridge Network is a limited company founded early in 1998 by a group of six organizations – 3i, Amadeus, Analysys Ltd, Arthur Andersen, N.W. Brown, and Cambridge University. The Cambridge Network enables its members to work together and leverage their collective resources in new ways for the benefit of technology-enabled enterprise and adjacent stakeholders in the Cambridge region in the UK. This is achieved by using a variety of technology, knowledge, and people-based tools to enhance business processes both on a local and a global scale. The network aims to achieve the highest standards in quality of service in order to uphold the traditions and sustain the progress of the "Cambridge Phenomenon." Professor Sir Alec Broers, vice-chancellor of the University of Cambridge and chairman of Cambridge Network, says that "the Cambridge Region is thriving because ways are being found to harness the amazing creative energy of those in the University and in business and turn their ideas to reality.

The Cambridge Network provides the ideal environment in which the links that allow this to happen can be forged. The Network offers a forum where people can get to know each other and discover how they can work together."

Link

www.cambridgenetwork.co.uk

LONDON BUSINESS SCHOOL INNOVATION FORUM

The London Business School Innovation Forum is a UK-based organization, linked to the London Business School, where members are able to engage in discussions, exchange ideas and information, and seek advice on issues related to innovation. Experts are brought in to contribute to leading-edge debate and ensure that latest management thinking and developments are brought into the Innovation Forum.

The Innovation Forum has been designed in response to feedback from the practicing managers and chief executives committed to innovation in their businesses. It provides a place in which to be imaginative and creative; a place that offers access to comprehensive and regularly updated resources; and a place to gain access to practical help.

It is a forum for sharing ideas through informal liaison and peer group discussions and offers an extensive range of resource material that is constantly updated. The Forum addresses emerging innovation issues on behalf of its members and can represent its members' interests through a wide network of contacts and associations.

In addition to the resources available remotely and on-site, the Forum runs seminars and workshops for its members on a range of themes relating to innovation to encourage peer group review and informal exchange of ideas and experiences.

Link

www.lbs.ac.uk

CRANFIELDCREATES

Based in the Cranfield School of Management in the UK, Cranfield-Creates provides advice, expertise, and resources to help individual entrepreneurs, early-stage growing businesses, and corporate clients build new e-business and technology-enabled ventures rapidly and successfully.

Cranfield School of Management became the first business school in Europe to assist MBA students in becoming e-business entrepreneurs when the Internet-business incubator, CranfieldCreates, was launched in January 2001.

Link

www.cranfieldcreates.com

THE STRATEGOS INSTITUTE

Linked to Strategos, the consultancy, the Strategos Institute is a consortium of successful companies who are addressing the business challenge of how to embed a deep, systemic capacity for innovation in large companies.

During its first two years, representatives from about 20 companies have worked both as a group and in intensive sub-teams, to pioneer new ways of inventing, testing, scaling, and leveraging innovative, wealth-creating strategies. They were guided and supported by the Institute's own staff and by a Research Advisory Board comprising leading business innovators and professors from the world's premier business schools. The consortium has created a blueprint for strategy innovation that encompasses the tools, metrics, processes, and climate that must be put in place to drive strategy innovation and new wealth-creation in an increasingly uncertain and complex world. This blueprint includes:

» a framework for understanding the role of strategy innovation in the creation of new wealth;
» tools for assessing the decay of an existing business strategy and the threats to its profit stream;
» new ways to think about industries and competitive domains that identify potential threats and white-space opportunities;
» insights into the organizational preconditions that must be created for innovation to flourish;

» a diagnostic for pinpointing the impediments to strategy innovation in any organization;

» a set of practical levers which management can use to stimulate new thinking, test new business models, and scale them up so that they become major revenue and profit contributors; and

» new performance measures designed to monitor a company's success in creating and capturing new wealth faster than its competitors.

Link

http://institute.strategosnet.com

CGEY CENTER FOR BUSINESS INNOVATION

The Cap Gemini Ernst & Young Center for Business Innovation discovers and develops innovations in strategy, organization, and technology to deliver high value. The group collaborates with leading thinkers in business, academia, and other research institutions. The research is used to aid the development of new strategic consulting services aimed at a general business audience.

Based in Boston, Massachusetts, more than 500 business executives visit the Center annually to participate in research, and to share information and experience. The Center also publishes a variety of research and consulting methods that benefit a wide audience.

Link

www.cbi.cgey.com

JOURNAL OF PRODUCT INNOVATION MANAGEMENT

The *Journal of Product Innovation Management* is the leading academic journal in the field and is dedicated to the advancement of management practice in all of the functions involved in the total process of product innovation. Its purpose is to bring to managers and students of product innovation the theoretical structures and the practical techniques that will enable them to operate at the cutting-edge of effective management practice. The scope is broad, taking account of those issues that are crucial to successful product innovation in the organization's external as well as internal environment. The intent is to be informative, thought provoking, and intellectually challenging, and thereby to contribute to the development of better managers.

The journal takes a multi-functional, multi-disciplinary, international approach to the issues facing those for whom product innovation is an important concern. It presents the research, experiences, and insights of academics, consultants, practicing managers, economists, scientists, lawyers, sociologists, and thoughtful contributors from other professions and disciplines. Since approaches to product innovation often differ in different economies and cultures, the journal draws on the work of authors from all over the world. Articles are based on empirical research, observations of management experience, and state-of-the-art reviews of important issues as well as conceptual and theoretical developments.

Link
www.jpim-online.com

TECHNOLOGY REVIEW

Published by MIT, the *Technology Review* is a leading magazine providing insights into new technologies and emerging applications. With regular contributions from leading scientists as well as major business personalities, the *Technology Review* provides a clear, objective, and authoritative point of view on issues that will impact future ideas.

Link
http://www.technologyreview.com

RED HERRING

Launched in 1993, *Red Herring* magazine provides a forward-thinking, analytical look at technology companies and industries, and evaluates technology as a strategic asset. *Red Herring* magazine's content seeks to be timely, analytical, and skeptical. It aims to tell its readers "what's first, what's new, and, most importantly, what matters."

Link
www.redherring.com

Ten Steps for Taking Ideas to Market

How do you actually improve your capability to successfully take ideas to market? This final chapter outlines the key aspects that you need to focus on:

» define a balanced innovation strategy;
» create an open and supportive culture;
» leverage all stakeholders to generate ideas;
» conduct efficient idea assessment and selection;
» use a clearly defined but flexible generic process;
» provide clear accountability and empower the team;
» focus on value generation;
» always pilot and test;
» ensure effective launch management; and
» don't forget post-launch learning reviews.

1. DEFINE A BALANCED INNOVATION STRATEGY

Before kicking off any idea generation, before building a team, and well before determining any launch plans, the first and critical step in taking ideas to market is to clearly determine the strategy, focus, and rationale. Some organizations rush into developing new products and services only to discover that the value that they thought was there for the taking is non-existent. Others create new offerings which, although full of promise and certainly an opportunity, are not applicable to the organization's capabilities to support and deliver. Successful firms take the time up-front to identify what arenas they want to play in and what the implications of this are. This not only provides focus for the organization but also avoids wastage and improves the chances of success.

The strategy itself is typically more successful if there is a balance of risk. Although many are drawn by the excitement of the radically new, there has to be recognition that chances of success are inherently smaller than with incrementalism. Likewise, although small step-change ideas are easier to both identify and deliver, the rewards that stand to be gained are far less than with something novel and definitive. Therefore, it is beneficial to ensure that a mix of high- and low-risk ideas is sought and supported by the organization, and to also provide the mechanism to manage this mix throughout their life cycles. Effective management of a portfolio of ideas from conception to implementation is hence an associated requirement. In addition, whereas in the past focus on one or more areas for idea exploitation was seen as key, as more and more organizations have moved from products into services and the provision of solutions, maintaining a view on opportunities for diversification is also important. Using objective assessments of project opportunity and viability throughout helps to drive prioritization of focus and effort as well as to ensure a supportive resource mix.

Lastly, to maintain a clear overview of how the ideas that are being developed and launched fit with the defined strategy, and to understand how well they are contributing to the overall objectives, many firms use some type of scoreboarding techniques to measure past, present, and future performance. In some industries, e.g. telecoms, the focus is more on the direct "here-and-now" with metrics such as average revenue per user as a key driver of determining success, whereas in others, like pharmaceuticals, it is the future potential and the value of the pipeline that is paramount.

2. CREATE AN OPEN AND SUPPORTIVE CULTURE

The other prerequisite for successful innovation in any organization is an appropriate and supportive culture. The environments within which ideas can be generated, developed, and implemented are in some ways different, but they are all a mile away from the traditional make-and-sell world of production lines and sales channels. Steady-state activities require focus on consistency, repetition, precision, and control, whereas the culture for innovation is one of experimentation, risk, and questioning, where uncertainty and ambiguity may prevail for a time. Although the two can exist in harmony in many organizations, the significance of creating the right environment for ideas to flourish cannot be understated.

Foremost, there is a need for openness. Both in terms of communication and access, an open environment is the single most important factor in stimulating creativity. Barriers, whether physical, such as walls, different buildings, or dispersed geographies, or organizational, such as hierarchies, functional silos, and secrecy, are killers of innovation and are difficult to overcome. Technologies such as e-mail, videoconferencing and intranets can partially help with the problems of multi-site working, but as yet, despite the hype, there is no artificial mechanism for recreating, in a virtual manner, the benefits that are gained from a true multi-disciplinary open environment where free interaction can successfully occur.

Underpinning this openness, there must also be an effective stimulus-motivation-reward mechanism operating throughout the organization to set the challenge and focus linked to the strategic direction, and to ensure a high level of engagement of all stakeholders within and outside the company. Achievement should be recognized through both financial and, even more significantly, non-financial means. In addition, learning from success and failure, both in the form of training in core capabilities and continuous reviews, to ensure knowledge and experience sharing, has to be taken seriously and not treated as a secondary activity. Lastly, and arguably most importantly, for enabling and driving the creation and continued evolution of an open culture, is the need for regular communication of the latest insights to the right people at the most appropriate level, together with the opportunity for quick and effective feedback.

3. LEVERAGE ALL STAKEHOLDERS TO GENERATE IDEAS

With a defined innovation strategy and supportive culture in place, the first core stage in taking ideas to market is clearly the generation of the candidate ideas themselves. Although some find it easy to conceive the next big thing, for most having ideas other than the obvious next step is a difficult hurdle. This is for many a key barrier to progress. However, through adopting and adapting a number of core techniques and approaches for stimulating and facilitating idea generation within an organization, and providing suitable training with sufficient provocation and challenge, ideas will flow. Moreover, by proactively engaging all stakeholders across, and external to, the organization, from suppliers, vendors, and subcontractors through to distributors, retailers, customers, end-users, and commentators, the source of potential new ideas can be significantly enhanced. Whether through focused cross-disciplinary brainstorms, individual creativity techniques, suggestion schemes, or customer interviews, any organization can affect a major in-flow of new ideas into the innovation funnel.

Paramount to any idea generation activity is a common focus for their collation. Not knowing where to send new ideas is a common issue in many firms that correspondingly leads to things just sitting in a bottom drawer gathering dust. People need to know where to address any ideas that they, their colleagues, or any external contacts propose. Whether an individual, group, or even a department, whoever is responsible for idea collection and collation has to be visible and perform at or above expectations – having a slow response for any ideas that are fed into a process kills enthusiasm and disengages the organization from innovation. A well-known airline had a suggestion scheme which promised quick feedback and assessment for any ideas that came in from its staff. However, with a typical delay of up to six months for even the initial acknowledgement of receipt, it was not long before it slipped from leader to copycat in an industry where innovation, particularly in customer service, is a key differentiator in the consumer purchase decision. Successful innovation companies place much importance on a response to new ideas that is fast and where open feedback on the benefits and the concerns associated with the idea can be discussed.

Lastly, every idea has to be allowed to be built upon and developed. Rarely is the first concept the same as the end product or service, but the seed of the idea is probably in there somewhere. Companies who are successful innovators often provide either the innovator or a concept team with the opportunity to take good ideas a few steps forward through discussing it with colleagues, customers, and other stakeholders so that, before full assessment, its true potential can be explored.

4. CONDUCT EFFICIENT IDEA ASSESSMENT AND SELECTION

It is with the need to evaluate and select the best ideas that companies encounter their next major problem. There is a balance between enabling sufficient development and building of ideas and being prepared to terminate ideas early on. Typically, only 1% of ideas ever make it through to launch and then, even in the best companies, only half of these are considered successful. As ideas move forward, the effort, resource, and hence money invested in them, increases significantly and so early filtering out of the losers is clearly attractive. However, too harsh a filter may well result in throwing out a concept that, with a bit of development, could have been a potential winner. Companies such as Siemens are increasingly introducing a quick filter approach up front, just after idea collation, which aims to take out between 50% and 75% of suggestions. They do this by having a few core killer criteria against which all ideas have to score positively in order to progress. These are the "must-haves" with which any opportunities that will deliver value to the company have to comply. Example criteria include the following.

» Is there a market for this idea?
» Does it fit with our corporate strategy?
» Do we have the capabilities to develop this idea?
» Will this idea potentially create value for the company?

One "no" stops progression but "yes" and "maybe" enables ideas to go through to the next level of assessment. By using this type of approach, firms can focus their evaluation efforts more wisely and expend resource investigating the opportunities that are more likely to make it. In addition, with such clear up-front criteria for progression, a certain degree of self-evaluation by the idea generators themselves can occur, which helps reduce non-viable suggestions and, at the same time, gives greater focus on the key needs and challenges ahead.

The second phase of this step is therefore a more detailed evaluation of the ideas that have passed the quick filter and have been developed further. Questions such as technological feasibility, size of market potential, likely return, partner dependency, intellectual property position, resource requirement, likely development time, and time-to-market, all have to be answered. These clearly become easier to address as ideas evolve and there is a higher degree of certainty, but sometimes a guesstimate up-front is far more effective than too much precision. Taking anything from two weeks to two months in the better companies, this key investigation is critical to future successful progression of the idea to market. Although this should not expand into such a high level of detail that it ends up taking forever to complete, thorough idea evaluation cannot be underestimated in its importance. While some wish to rush through ideas in order to capitalize on the opportunity as soon as possible, two weeks spent investigating the idea here can save six to twelve months needed for fixing problems later on.

The last phase in this step is the ever-difficult activity of idea selection. It is here that emotional and political influences raise their ugly heads. After time spent building and assessing any idea, it is not surprising that enthusiasm builds. Idea selection has to be objective, ignore emotions and politics, and focus on the purely rational. Again, clearly defined and agreed criteria are the key in this activity as they enable idea ranking and prioritization, drive the selection decision, and determine which to progress into the next stage.

5. USE A CLEARLY DEFINED BUT FLEXIBLE GENERIC PROCESS

No matter how good the idea and thorough the evaluation, getting it from a developed concept through to launch and beyond is no easy task.

If it is a product-based idea, aspects such as the overall product architecture, components, interfaces, aesthetic form, functional reliability, and performance all have to be defined, tested, and their mutual interaction and dependency evaluated. If it is a service-based idea, issues such as service descriptions at market, product and technology levels, all have to be defined, and IT systems required for delivery, maintenance, billing, and replacement need to be determined, and service-level agreements must be established and agreed with partners. In addition, no matter whether a product or service, marketing campaigns need to be defined, sales forces trained, contracts prepared, and pricing strategies defined. In all, this can become a highly complex challenge involving numerous different functions and organizations demanding a significant level of coherent and effective project management. Underpinning and enabling this is the need for a clearly defined, flexible, yet disciplined, process for taking ideas from conception through to hand-over into a steady-state organization. This is the fifth key step in taking ideas to market.

Although many fear the bureaucracy and lethargy of complex processes, there is little doubt that, at some level, a commonly understood, accessible, and inclusive process is critical. Essentially, everything detailed above is a series of decisions – some complex, some simple. Coherent decision-making throughout the process is therefore a critical success factor. This decision-making is necessarily linked into the individual tasks that need to occur to bring together the varied elements to deliver the idea. However, at a high level, there are really only three key decisions and these can serve as major review points for each and every project.

While terminology varies from industry to industry and from firm to firm, development approval – the decision to kick off a major project and move from concept to reality; launch approval – the decision to first introduce the new idea to the market; and general availability – the point where everything required to support and operate the product or service is fully in place; are the three core points where an organization can assess progress. These are the points where transition from one phase to another is determined. They are also the points where projects can be stopped – either temporarily or permanently. Termination of a development program is the ever-present issue that all companies have difficulty dealing with. Once kicked off, a project can easily develop such momentum that it cannot be stopped but, if the market changes, if competitors introduce a better idea, or if new technology renders the idea redundant, it has to be stopped and these three major decision points provide firms with the ability to do so in an objective and apolitical manner.

Lastly, underpinning any process is the enabler of metrics and key performance indicators. Measures such as time-to-market, time-to-profit, resource utilization and budget spend are all key drivers on an effective idea delivery process and, if monitored, also provide the mechanism for the decision-making required.

6. PROVIDE CLEAR ACCOUNTABILITY AND EMPOWER THE TEAM

Accountability throughout the creation, selection, and delivery phases of taking an idea to market is a fundamental issue. Without sufficient responsibility, a development team becomes disempowered and will not have enough authority to overcome the inevitable obstacles that it encounters. With too much autonomy, any group has the potential to veer away from the intended path and fail. The secret, just as with the overall innovation strategy, is balance. This can best be articulated through the definition and agreement of a comprehensive accountability model covering the whole development process. Individual groups within the overall development program have to be given responsibility for their respective tasks and the freedom to determine the most appropriate solution, but this has to occur within a coherent structure where overall accountability resides with an identified project leader, service director, or product manger. Someone has to have the authority to approve budget, resolve conflicts, prioritize options and, if necessary, terminate a project. This has to be someone who is not only knowledgeable about the idea, its market, the challenges as well as the organizations involved in its realization, but also has to be respected by both the team and senior management. Without this, problems occur only too easily.

Organization is part of the context of good innovation governance. Generally, organizational form should follow strategic intent. If the intent is to develop radically new businesses, with the potential to

IPO as separate entities, then the most appropriate organizational form is likely to be an incubator unit, with very little linkage to the core, heritage businesses. Where the intent is to develop radical new products or businesses that draw strongly on heritage assets in the main businesses (assets like brands, people, technologies, or processes), then the best form will be a separate unit but with at least dotted-line accountability into the core businesses. By contrast, if the intent is to incrementally improve existing products and processes, the best structure is to base the team within existing marketing, product development, or business improvement teams.

In addition, the level of overall senior management involvement is a key issue in enabling successful progression. Too much interference results in changing priorities, politics, and an increasing role for the chairman's entourage. Too little support and gaining the necessary input and commitment across the organization becomes a never-ending obstacle for the development team. Yet again, it is an issue of balance. Senior management should be involved in decision-making but only in the three key review points of development approval, launch approval, and general availability. Here they can air their views and influence the outcome, but between these points they are only involved if required either to deal with an escalated issue or for strategic counsel. Their support and confidence in the idea together with clear endorsement of the team is critical but their willingness to delegate and allow those tasked with undertaking the necessary component activities to get on with it without interference is essential.

7. FOCUS ON VALUE GENERATION

Throughout the whole process of taking any idea to market, a clear and consistent focus on value is perhaps one of the most significant differentiators between the leaders and the rest of the pack. Value, for the customer, for the provider, and for any partners, is a key issue. It is a core driver underpinning a purchase decision, it determines and directly impacts many internal measures of success, and it encourages suppliers, distributors, and other stakeholders to continue to work with you. As such, how much value is being generated, where from, by whom and, most significantly, how it is being shared, has to be tracked throughout the journey from concept to reality. This is easier said than done.

Up-front, during the strategic and idea assessment phases, the value that will be generated and delivered by any individual idea is highly visible. It drives the enthusiasm for taking it forward and, as a key element of most selection processes, helps to dictate whether or not it ever gets the go-ahead. However, once underway, the value, and specifically the relative value of one idea to another, can become obscured as they inevitably fight for attention, resource, and prioritization. The decisions taken along the development journey can significantly impact the magnitude and sharing of value and hence what was promised may well not be delivered.

There are many ways of measuring value and its importance can vary from industry to industry. Across all sectors, many find it useful to look at the value being created and potentially available across a portfolio of ideas in an objective and, sometimes abstract, manner. A favorite in some companies is to consider all ideas as trees in an orchard vying for attention and resource. While it may be easy to continue to support the apple tree that has been growing for years, it could be wiser to share some effort with the lemon tree which, although smaller, could generate more value – after all, lemons may generate 10 times the value of apples. In addition, when things get tight as the market changes or new technology is introduced, the organization may be better off forgetting the apple tree, even though it is nearly ready to bear fruit, as figs may well have become the next big thing and the fig tree that has been left alone over in the corner surrounded by weeds could be ready to deliver value shortly. This and similar metaphors help companies think objectively, focus on where the true value lies and allocate and switch effort accordingly.

8. ALWAYS PILOT AND TEST

The days when a product could be launched and any problems resolved afterwards are far gone. One poor review of a newly launched product significantly, and possibly permanently, damages any chance of success – look at what happened to the A-class Mercedes when it failed to navigate a hypothetical elk! A product withdrawal was followed by a 12-month improvement program to introduce electronic compensation and a full product relaunch. Fixing problems after launch is costly and can significantly damage both product and brand. Product recalls, bugs in software, and poor reviews are all killers of value and major obstacles to success. The solution to this? Piloting – introducing a new idea into an incubator environment with a lead customer. No matter whether developing a new financial service or a new car, to iron out the glitches in any new product or service, companies are increasingly using beta-test environments to soft-launch their new ideas, try out options, and determine which work best. Examples of this in practice include Egg and Virgin Atlantic.

Egg, a UK-based Internet bank, had pioneered high-interest savings accounts via the Internet and wished to make a move into the higher value world of investment trusts. The company's supermarket concept brought together 40-plus providers and allows their customers to pick and choose where to invest their money within an overall portfolio with the essence being on individual management and reduced fees from collective purchasing. Faced with a major launch of a new product into a highly competitive environment, Egg chose to run a controlled pilot with 100 sample customers for a month, simulating investment and access to funds. Trying out user interface, sales support, IT systems, together with lead-consumer validation, this exercise cost relatively little but provided the organization with the opportunity to debug their software, check customer care procedures, and clarify interface protocols so that the subsequent hard-launch to an eager yet critical customer base was an unqualified success.

Similarly, Virgin Atlantic was faced with a key decision for their new Upper Class seating. Having successfully acquired many new customers from British Airways, United and American Airlines, with their superior service and more competitive pricing, the company wanted to introduced a major innovation into their fleet but wanted to check the impact before launch. Virgin had a highly innovative radical design of seat that was planned to be introduced. Before Virgin went ahead with roll-out, they first conducted a month of controlled tests in a simulator where carefully selected customers spent a night "flying to New York" in the new seat and an alternative, less radical, design. The results of this piloting gave Virgin both valuable feedback on customer likes and dislikes and the confidence to go for a full launch across the fleet. In the end Virgin chose the radical design, won praise, design awards, and even more customer recognition for innovation.

Organizations like Accenture use their Interactive Design Group to co-ordinate the design work for the e-services they develop, and to undertake specific pre-launch evaluation using actual target customers. In particular, they achieve the best possible customer focus by seamlessly integrating all the disparate components of an effective design – creative, technical, marketing, usability, content – and testing the outputs with customers at various stages along the way. This reduces the risk of building technically brilliant Websites with unfriendly technology or little clear benefit to consumers.

9. ENSURE EFFECTIVE LAUNCH MANAGEMENT

Step 9 is focused on the management of the product launch. For pharmaceutical companies where development projects can take up to 10 years, dedicated launch teams to co-ordinate the introduction of a new drug into multiple markets take control of new products for a period of a year before and after official release. However, in most companies, product launch is conducted either by product marketing, sales, or, in some cases, the development team. Going back 20 years, the introduction of a new idea into a local market was a comparatively easy exercise focused on co-ordination of advertising, marketing collateral, and product introduction. Today, when more and more firms launch simultaneously over multiple geographies, things are far more complicated.

When, for example, a European telecoms firm has to launch a new service across 20 countries within a two-week timeframe, issues such as local regulations, translations of sales kits into 15 different languages, training of sales teams, co-ordinating 18 different advertising campaigns, and a cascading product availability, all supported by the necessary local provisioning and IT support, ensuring a seamless and coherent introduction of the service without any glitches is a major task. More and more companies are recognizing that launch management is a specialist skill, one which combines an understanding of marketing with the reality of operational readiness, and something which, to effect an efficient introduction and minimize the risks of failure, they need to develop as a core capability.

10. DON'T FORGET POST-LAUNCH LEARNING REVIEWS

Finally, step 10 is focused on learning. Whether success or failure, the opportunities that stand to be gained from capturing the experiences and lessons learned, and then sharing them across the organization, are multiple. If successful, a new standard is defined. Best practice can become the norm and through conducting a post-launch review the new things that worked can be identified and the experiences captured. Similarly, if there is a failed launch, a postmortem helps identify what went wrong and provides focus for identifying how to avoid the same issues in the future. Whatever the outcome, taking a day to bring the team together and reflect on the experiences that they have shared is a valuable use of time for the individuals in terms of specific learning and for the organization in terms of knowledge-capture.

When undertaking such a review it is vital that it takes place in a constructive and objective environment and not one where either praise and self-congratulation or blame and criticism dominate. Although usually initially focused on the process and the procedures adopted for taking the idea to market and identifying the key learnings from this, it is often in the inter-relationships and cross-functional interfaces that the real insights are found. Once an idea has been assessed, chosen, and a good team provided to take it to launch, it can generally follow a pretty generic and predictable process. What makes this work and differentiates between success and failure is the interaction between the various parties throughout the process. Dealing with issues such as frequency of communication, detail of information, level of trust and respect, are frequently the softer elements in a successful project that come out in a post-launch review. It is these people-based skills and capabilities which need to be fed back into the rest of the organization and integrated into working practice to ensure future success and continued improvement.

KEY LEARNING POINTS

» Up-front, the strategy, focus, and rationale for any ideas have to be determined and clearly communicated.

» A prerequisite for success is a supportive culture in which experimentation, risk, and questioning are encouraged; it is a culture in which ambiguity can prevail.

» By proactively engaging stakeholders from within the organization and external to it, the source of potential new ideas can be greatly enhanced.

» Effective early filtering of ideas is increasingly important. A focus on value-delivery from ideas, through clearly defined and agreed criteria, should drive the assessment.

» Enabling the taking of ideas from concept through to the launch of a final product, or service, has to be supported by a clearly defined, flexible, yet disciplined, process.

» Development teams should be empowered throughout the process – the objective is a balance of autonomy and responsibility.

» The value being created through the evolution of an idea has to be tracked throughout the development phase.

» Rectifying problems in products or services post-launch can be expensive. Piloting products and services is crucial in determining what will work best and be what the end users want.

» Launch management has to be recognized as a separate skill, and needs to be developed as a core capability to minimize the risk of failure in the launch-to-market.

» The opportunities that stand to be gained from capturing experiences and lessons learnt are many. An approach should be integrated to continued improvement.

Frequently Asked Questions (FAQs)

Q1: Why is taking ideas to market important?

A: See Chapter 1, Introduction.

Q2: How do I come up with more good ideas?

A: See Chapter 2, Idea creation, Chapter 10, Steps 2 and 3.

Q3: How do I choose which ideas are the winners?

A: See Chapter 2, Idea selection Chapter 10, Steps 1 and 4.

Q4: How can the Internet help me innovate?

A: See Chapter 4, The E-Dimension.

Q5: How do I better motivate people?

A: See Chapter 7, In Practice, 3M and Skandia, and Chapter 10, Step 2.

Q6: How can we improve our performance?

A: See Chapter 3, Evolution of Ideas to Market, Chapter 6, State of the Art, and Chapter 10, Ten Steps for Taking Ideas to Market.

Q7: How do I best organize my team?

A: See Chapter 5, The Global Dimension, and Chapter 10, Step 6.

Q8: Where can I go for help?

A: See Chapter 9, Resources.

Q9: Who are the experts in taking ideas to market?

A: See Chapter 7, In Practice, and Chapter 8, Key Concepts and Thinkers.

Q10: What are the critical success factors for taking ideas to market?

A: See Chapter 3, Idea delivery.

Acknowledgments

The authors would like to thank Anna Soisalo for her patience, encouragement, input, editing and feedback.

We would like to dedicate this book to Rich Gabriel, whose wisdom, wit and friendship were lost too soon.

Index

Printed and bound in the UK by
CPI Antony Rowe, Eastbourne

Printed and bound by CPI Group (UK) Ltd, Croydon, CR0 4YY

13/04/2025

14656560-0002